Death to the Bishop

John G. Pisarcik

ISBN 978-1-64003-509-6 (Paperback)
ISBN 978-1-64003-510-2 (Digital)

Covenant Books, Inc.
11661 Hwy 707
Murrells Inlet, SC 29576
www.covenantbooks.com

Contents

Introduction

My name is John Writerson. I am a Roman Catholic priest. My present assignment is as master of ceremonies and priest-secretary to the Most Rev. William Harrington, bishop of the Diocese of Wallington.

The following is how I remember the events that took place and how we responded to them at the time. Usually, at night before I retire, I dictate my thoughts and make a file. That data automatically is recorded on my computer and ready for me to read, add, or subtract material at a later date.

I have tried to show them in the order in which they happened. However, since events span over six years that I have lived and worked with Bishop Harrington and are my personal recollections, I do jump around at times, as one event reminds me of another that took place. Hopefully, that will not be a great distraction to you. Bear with me, it will be worth your time and effort. I know it has been an incredible journey for me.

Chapter 1

It was a raw winter evening, and the snow had just started to fall, the small flake type that promises a large snowfall by morning. He stood alone, tall, with stately bearing, black cashmere overcoat buttoned to the neck, warding off the cold. Black fedora covering his pure white hair. Smoke rising from the pipe he furiously puffed on as he contemplates the latest threat against his life. Already having lived sixty-eight years, he was not afraid of dying, in many ways looking forward to death. For as long as he could remember, he had professed that he believed in the dead experiencing an afterlife. Tonight, however, everything seemed to be different. Things were happening so fast, changes taking place with unforeseeable consequences and he was in charge. Being bishop of this diocese was no small task in regular times, but these were not regular at all. And so, the Most Reverend Walter B. Harrington found himself alone, standing in the cold, snow swirling around him, wondering how much time he had left.

Life had been much simpler when he was ordained a priest and later when ordained a bishop. Roles were clear, respect was given, a hierarchy was an accepted way of life. The Second Council of the Vatican changed much of that, at least as far as the people were concerned. They no longer genuflected to kiss his ring when he came to the local parishes to administer the Sacrament of Confirmation or special ceremonies. No, everyone just wanted to shake hands or have those blasted selfie pictures taken with him. His Irish wit made him a popular speaker throughout the diocese. People enjoyed his sense of humor and down-to-earth approach when chatting with their sons and daughters. Bishop Harrington was a popular fundraiser for Capital Campaigns or diocesan drives.

Bishop Harrington liked to believe that he was always available to the priests of the diocese or people who requested to personally see him. Shortly after he arrived, to be bishop of this diocese, he had instructed his good secretary and guardian of the entrance to his office that anyone who called is given an appointment. However, he limited the time for each to fifteen minutes in length. Bishop Harrington felt that if they could not get to the point within the first fifteen minutes, it would prove to be a waste of time. Many resented the fact that before their seat was even warm, as visitors would tell, you were being ushered out of the office by

Rose, the same secretary who let you in. That policy would lay the foundation for the plot to kill him. There were too many in the community and diocese who believed they deserved more than his allotted fifteen minutes because of who they were or what they had done for the diocese.

Behind his back, he was often called the coal miner, because of the way he spoke out of the side of his mouth and the earthy tales he told. Bishop Walter Harrington naturally knew or had, over the years, heard himself called it to realize that he probably came across that way. Years of smoking that dang pipe of his, yes, had made it look like he was talking out of the right side of his mouth. It gave him a good laugh because he knew that he was not that rough, tough guy they believed him to be. Actually, Wally, as his close friends and fellow bishops called him, really was a gentle soul. He loved golf, admittedly not good at it, as well as a good game of cards. Vacations were always filled with days of golf and rounds of cards in the evening, with a brandy on the table, sharing stories, jokes with lifelong friends.

Tonight, was not a night of comfort, but anxiety. He did not feel safe, even in this stately old house left to the diocese for the use of its bishop. If he chooses not to live in it, the house will revert back to the family of the original owner. Bishop Harrington made his way back into the warmth of the house, leaving his overcoat on the rake by the door. Slowly he climbed the steps to the second floor and to his study/home office. He loved this room. With its large windows overlooking the city, the bookcases lining the walls, the overstuffed furniture that even accommodated his six-foot-two stature. Here he felt at ease. Wally loved writing and did most of his here in this study rather than the official office in the chancery building. He always believed if he had not been a priest and bishop, he would love to have been a writer. And so, it was when he was here, where there were no distractions, he had complete peace.

Over the last six months, he had received six death threats. From time to time, almost all his colleagues who were bishops had experienced letters from disgruntled individuals or priests. Most were just that, a letter written out of frustration, a venting of momentary anger at the man who was at the top of the local hierarchy. These messages were different in nature, tone, and intent. He had debated handing them over to the local police but had decided not to do that at this time. If there was a way he could reach this person, maybe he could be the healer he was sent to be. A good shepherd who looked after even those who were lost and carried them back into the fold. Going over the six communique for the tenth time still gave him no clue as to whom the person or persons might be. All he knew was that there was great anger expressed in each one of the six messages.

Harrington reached over and hit the intercom button. When it clicked, he asked me to come into his study. My name is Father John Writerson, and I am the bishop's priest secretary, master of ceremonies, right-hand man. If you see him in public, I will be the priest standing off to his right, ever ready to pick up on any signal from him. It is my job to make sure things run smoothly, liturgically correct, and on time. Bishop is a real stickler for time. He does not like being late, kept waiting for a ceremony to start, or asked to engage in idle conversation. This is my fifth year doing the job. I live here in the residence of the bishop, accompany him on all official business and make sure that everything he will need for a ceremony has been properly packed and in the car. The longtime driver for whomever the bishop is, Fred McNamara, has been in his job close to twenty-two years now. I depend on him a great deal because of his experience, his knowledge of the places we are going to be visiting, and the personnel assigned to them.

As soon as I entered the study, I could tell something was bothering the Boss from his facial expression and the way he was sitting in his favorite chair. Usually, he sat very upright, but tonight he was slouched in it, most unlike him. Plus, I noticed how weary he looked. We have had a kind of busy schedule, with holiday affairs, administration of the Sacrament of Confirmation in twelve parishes over the last two weeks takes its toll. I am thirty-some years younger than the bishop, and I feel somewhat exhausted. Yet I have to admit, looks like more than exhaustion from keeping up with our schedule.

The first thing he does is invite me to sit down in the chair next to him. I can only recall one other time he asked me to do that, and it was to tell me that he just received a phone call informing him that his beloved mother Margaret had died. Naturally, a sense of foreboding crept over me as I sat down in the overstuffed chair. Quietly he handed over to me six papers. Bishop asked if I would read through them and tell him what I thought. When I began to read the content of the letters, I knew I was out of my league. This is not what I was trained for or hired to handle for him. He trusted me like a father would his oldest son to give him a straight answer. Gradually, I put the six papers down on the little table that was between the two chairs. After a moment, I looked at him and said I thought he should call the station and ask for Detective James Teeling. He was not only head of the detective bureau but also a regular parishioner at the cathedral parish. I knew he would know what to do and how to do it discreetly. To my surprise, Bishop said he would not do that.

Being concerned for his welfare, safety, and that of those around him, I asked him why.

He looked at me with sad eyes and said that in some ways, he felt whoever this person was that they were correct in many respects. We had both read the same six letters and apparently saw something different. I saw a clear threat to the life of our bishop. I read the words that were filled with anger toward the Church in general and about him in particular. For the life of me, I could not see how the Boss did not see the same thing.

We sat there in silence for a time, I have no idea now how long it actually was before he spoke. "John, you have been at my side for some years now, a priest I could count on to make sure everything ran smooth, but in our effort to make the diocese more efficient, we may have missed important signs of discontent." Bishop then asked me to make copies of the six communique and take a copy to my room and study them as he had been doing since they arrived.

"What was common, if anything besides the angry tone, in all six of them? How was this person so deeply hurt that he or she felt that only in taking my life would the pain go away? If we can figure that out, maybe we can reach out to this person through the diocesan newspaper or some means to set up a meeting. My role is to not only to shepherd this diocese but to be a means of reconciliation, forgiveness, and a sign of God's mercy toward His people. Apparently, at least with this writer, I have failed miserably in that task. Be assured, John, that I will also seriously consider your suggestion that we get Detective Teeling discreetly involved, I do not want to see anyone hurt if it can be avoided."

Needless to say, I did not sleep that night. Constantly tossing and turning, my mind filled with grisly images of how this person intended to carry out the threat. Now I understood why Bishop has looked so tired as of late. If I cannot sleep, how much more has this weighed upon him? One thing I knew for sure was that at some point, we were going to have to get Detective Jimmy in here and give us some guidance on what we should or should not be doing. I knew Harrington would not stop his pastoral responsibility of visiting the parishes, confirming our youth, attending endless civic and church meetings throughout the diocese. Nor, I knew, would he ever agree that his monthly schedule not be published. All bishops believed the people have a right to know where they would be during the month. So Bishop's schedule is out there for anyone to come out to see him, interact with him, or just have their picture taken with him. There is no doubt in my mind that this nightmare was way beyond my pay grade.

The next morning, after we had celebrated Mass in the chapel of the residence, we had our breakfast. No mention was made about last night. We were back to our daily routine and a busy week ahead of us. The residence has two religious women from the Order of the Cross living in it. One takes care of meals when we are home, and the other takes care of housekeeping and laundry. The two of them have served four bishops now and did not intend retiring. And to that, we both said, "Thanks be to God!" Sometimes Bishop would get frustrated with Sister Kunegunda, OC, because she would scold him for not correctly folding his ceremonial attire after a religious event, and she would have to press out all the wrinkles. No one knew how much he perspired under all those garments. The first thing Bishop did after a parish ceremony was head to the pastor's rooms and change his clothes. Either Fred, his driver, or I would towel him down as he stood there in the skivvies and hand him a dry undershirt, dress shirt, and clerical frontal. Once back in his suit jacket, he would head out and greet the priests and crowd who had gathered. Heaven help all of us, if we, in our rush, just threw those damp clothes and formal robes of the bishop just into the suitcase. None of us wanted to face Sr. Kunegunda, OC, when she was annoyed.

It was just 7:45 AM when Fred pulled the car out of the garage and we headed down to the chancery office. By 8:00 AM we were all in our respective offices. Bishop's secretary was always the first into see him after his arrival. She would go over the schedule for the day of who was coming into the office to see him, and if she had ascertained what it would be about. After that, Bishop Harrington always spent the next hour dictating correspondence for her to prepare for him to sign. Usually at nine fifteen, the first of the day's appointments would begin. Without fail, every fifteen minutes, the secretary would notify Bishop that his next appointment was waiting.

Most days we had lunch right there in the chancery cafeteria. Nothing lavish, usually soup, a sandwich or salad, a cup of tea, and then back to work. In all respects, today was no different than any other day at the office, except today I knew someone was out to kill our Boss.

Early in the morning, I talked to Rose, Bishop's lay secretary, if anyone had when calling for an appointment seemed overly angry, or in anyway threatening her or Bishop. Rose looked over the list for today and all of the week and told me there was only one individual that she really did not know and he was not coming in till Thursday. He had insisted on seeing the bishop personally and had been adamant on the phone about that fact. He did not want to see the Vicar-General of the diocese (second in command if you will) or me, his priest secretary, but Bishop himself. Rose had scheduled him for fifteen minutes on Thursday afternoon at 2:30 PM. I looked at the name, Martin Thompson, and it did not ring a bell with me as someone we had met at a recent gathering, fundraiser, or liturgical ceremony. I quickly jotted it down to do some research of my own on this person who was so adamant on seeing Bishop.

Around 4:00 PM, Fred brought the car to the entrance of the chancery, got out, and opened the back passenger side door for Bishop Harrington. I opened my own door and got in behind the driver. Like most nights, the Boss was going back to the residence with a stack of papers to be gone over before tomorrow. He would be putting in another long evening since at 7:30 PM, we were going to St. Ambrose parish on the south side of the city to celebrate their one hundredth anniversary of the founding of the church. They were having the evening Mass so parishioners who worked could attend and a dinner/dance was to be held on Saturday night after the regular 5:00 PM Mass.

Sister Anesia, OC, our cook and meal server, informed us that dinner would be at five thirty sharp. She then told Bishop that would give him time to take a short nap and change into a new suit before we would have to leave at six thirty. I, for one, just needed a quick shower to revive myself, get dressed, and sit down and pray vespers/evening prayer in our small chapel. At precisely five thirty, the dinner bell rang, and the two of us made our way down to the dining room. Because we had to go out this evening, Sister Anesia had made us a simple ham dinner with baked potatoes, mixed vegetables, hot rolls, and a glass of Pinot Noir. The food was done to perfection, and the wine felt good as it warmed both body and soul. We talked a little about his day, who he saw, and what actions he intended to take in light of the day's appointments. He asked me, probably for the 160th time now if I had sent the instruction sheet to the pastor as to what would be needed for the Mass. I assured him that I had indeed sent it and hoped he had gone over it with those who would be lectors, the two servers who would carry the bishop's miter and his crozier when he was not using them. It would be my responsibility to get them at the appropriate times, place the miter on his head, and hand him the crozier in his left hand.

Fred had the car ready for us and drove over to the south side of our city and St. Ambrose Rectory. The pastor, Father Henry Stalling, greeted us as we disembarked from the vehicle. He was a man in his early sixties, jovial type of guy, who was committed to inner-city work and the poor that he served.

When the parish was founded one hundred years ago, it was mainly a church-serving German immigrant families. Today, it was mostly Hispanic, Black, and German. Amazingly, the parish had been able to keep the elementary school financially sound for the last sixty years. In today's day and age, that is a major accomplishment in itself. The parishioners were committed to the Catholic education of their children, made the sacrifices necessary, and held many a fundraiser during the year. Bishop Harrington had attended quite a few of them, giving his support to their effort and commitment. However, tonight was a night of joyful celebration for the parish community.

The Mass went smoothly; the church had an overflow gathering. Many families coming back just to be here for this celebration. The Liturgy started about three minutes ahead of time, and I knew by the smile on his face that Bishop was utterly delighted. After the Liturgy, Bishop Harrington and Father Stalling stood outside the massive front doors and greeted the people as they came out. That alone took another forty minutes with all the picture-taking, sharing of short memories about the parish people wanted the bishop to know about.

We did not get home till after ten thirty and both of us were exhausted. Bishop and I both retired to our rooms for the night. I know I was asleep within a half hour's times. The next morning, he told me he went over those papers he brought home with him, so he did not get to bed for another hour and a half.

The next day, I decided to Google Martin Thompson. There was not much public information on this man. He was a self-made millionaire. How he made his money was not so clear from what I could find on the internet. It looked like he owned coin laundry stores in this state and three other states. There was one newspaper article about how he had proposed to the city council that churches be charged taxes and made to pay for property that was surrounding their buildings. He had maintained that the land the buildings sat on could be tax exempt but not all the land around them. In particular, he had pointed out the vast amount of land owned by the diocese and our parishes. Representatives of the diocese and other Christian denominations, as well as the Jewish and Muslim community all argued about the need for the tax exemption status to continue operating as charitable organizations. The article went on to say that the council chooses to allow the tax exemption status to stay as it was written.

I picked up the intercom and dialed Rose's number and asked her if she could get me into seeing Bishop for five minutes. She told me that there was a change in time for one appointment in the afternoon, and if I came down the hall, I could see him for the five minutes at two forty-five. Sharply at the appointed time, I entered his office. Needless to say, Bishop Harrington was surprised to see me standing in front of him. I came right to the point and asked him if he had given any further thought to having Detective Teeling see the letters and advise us on how to proceed. He looked at me and told me that he had and agreed that it would be best to seek his advice. The only condition was that if it could be kept confidential, he would appreciate it. I told him I would get on it right away.

When I went back to my office, I called the police station and asked for him directly. Since he is head of the department, he has a secretary. She told me that he was in a meeting with a team of detectives working on a murder case that has been in the news for the last couple of weeks. I asked her when he was free if he could give me a call here at the chancery or on my cell phone number, which I proceeded to give her.

Our schedule did not have anything on it for this evening. One of those rare nights when we were going to be free. I called one of my priest class-mates, and best friend, and asked Louis Santiago if he wanted to go to dinner or a movie this evening. Lou told me he could not make dinner, but he would be free by 7:00 PM, and if I could find something decent for us to see, he was game for going to the movies. The movie theater in the next town had one that started at seven thirty, and I knew we could both make it there on time. So I called Lou back and told him to meet me at the movie theater, and he said he was looking forward to it.

At three thirty-five my phone rang, and it was James Telling on the other end. As always, he came right to the point and asked why I was calling him and asked if I have information about our killer. I assured him that I did not, but I would like to see him at his earliest convenience but not here at the chancery or his office. Bells must have gone off in his detective's head, and he immediately asked why. I told him that it was important to Bishop Harrington that we keep everything confidential at this stage. Jimmy told me to inform the Boss that he would meet with him and me at Our Lady of Hope Cemetery on Saturday afternoon at two o'clock. He knew, as I did, by that time, there would be no burials scheduled and the workers would have gone home. Union rules had them finishing work at 12:00 PM on Saturdays. We agreed to meet at the cemetery chapel.

On our ride home to the residence, I told Bishop about the proposed meeting, and he agreed it was a right place since there would be virtually no one around. He asked if, before I went out with Father

Lou for the movies, I would make another copy of the six communique so that Detective Teeling would have a set for his own use. I told him I would take care of it as soon as we got back to the residence. We rode the rest of the way home in silence, both of us absorbed in our own thoughts.

Chapter 2

Here it is, Thursday morning, and we are all in our respective offices at the chancery building. Today is the day our mysterious Mr. Thompson will be coming in to see the bishop. I did alert our security guard to come to my office at one forty since I knew Thompson's appointment was for one forty-five today. That way, Henry, our security guard, would just be steps from the bishop's office should he be needed. In most cases, just his physical presence was enough to put the fear of God into an average person. Henry stood six feet, six inches and weighed in probably around 245 pounds of solid muscle. He was a very intimidating man, to say the least. I, for sure, would not want to run into him or be on his bad side. I would make sure to send him down to Rose's office where Mr. Thomson would be waiting so he could clearly see this hulk of a man and, hopefully, would have second thoughts if he was planning on trying to harm Bishop Harrington. Henry arrived at Rose's office just as she was about to lead

Thompson to the entrance door of the office of the bishop. As expected, Mr. Thompson took a real close look at Henry, and you could see an absolute respect in his eyes, or maybe fear at this new person.

Henry and I waited in Rose's office with her for the fifteen minutes to come and go. Bishop did have a hidden button on his desk that he could push if he felt his life was in danger. If he pushed it, a bell would go off in the security office, and red lights would go on in Rose's, the chancellor, Vicar-General, and my offices. We knew the drill; we had planned for it, practiced it among ourselves as to what we would do, who would enter first and what our response would be to an assortment of potential dangers the bishop could be in. Naturally, we all prayed and hoped the plans never had to be used. Since the Vicar-General is second in charge of the diocese, he had the only stun gun we owned. He had been trained by our local police on how to use it and would if it came to it being called for in a particular situation. I had flex cuffs for hands and feet and was prepared to quickly attach them if need be. The chancellor, who is the official secretary of the diocese, was there to make sure an accurate record would be taken of what happened, who participated, and what the outcome would be.

Today, the red light did not go off, and at the end of the fifteen minutes, Mr. Thompson left the office of the bishop to all of our relief. Henry went back to his post on the first floor, I immediately went into see what Mr. Thompson had wanted with the Boss. To my utter surprise, the bishop was sitting at his desk with a smile on his face and slightly shaking his head in bewilderment. He looked up at me and said I would never be able to guess what the meeting was about or what Thompson wanted. So he would only tell me. Mr. Thompson wanted nothing from the bishop or the diocese. He had no grievance against Bishop personally or the diocese. Bishop had stopped talking and was looking at the piece of paper he held in his hand, still shaking his head in disbelief. Finally, he said to me that the early years of life for Mr. Thompson were not productive or pleasant. His teenage years were filled with one temptation after another to join a street gang. He managed to ward off the gang pressure, rise above the other temptations to do drugs, become an abuser, and got himself an education. Now he wanted to give back. He had handed Bishop a check made out to the Diocese of Wallington for fifteen million dollars to be used for inner-city programs for the youth of the diocese. He envisioned after-school programs to keep kids off the streets and away from gangs. He could see the diocese building a rec center for basketball, racquetball, swimming under the supervision of diocesan staff. Bishop William Harrington, DD, Bishop of Wallington, had assured him that he would make sure the money went to those programs as well as meal programs. It was the largest gift by an individual the diocese had ever received, and it would be used as the donor wished. Bishop still could not believe his eyes as he gazed at the check and all the good it would be utilized for. Naturally, those programs would have to be funded in years to come and staff salaries budgeted, but he hoped that this check would be the motivation needed for others to step forward and offer financial support. The only real request Mr. Thompson had was that the diocese would not reveal who had given the money, expect that it was a local businessman who believed in this city, its youth, and for a brighter future.

We went home that evening elated at this generous gift and the good that it would produce over the next few years. It would take at least two years to construct the recreation center that Thompson envisioned with basketball, racquetball courts, and a swimming pool. We saw a second building housing the afterschool rooms and a cafeteria that would be able to provide a balanced meal for those low-income families who might not be able to afford otherwise. So many of the parents worked more than one job that often there was no one at home when the children would arrive. In most cases, they would have to prepare their own supper if there was anything in the house for them to eat. This monetary gift of Mr. Thompsons's would significantly impact their lives for years to come. Not only would they have a safe place to go after school, but a hot meal would also be available to them.

Friday seemed to fly by for me. Bishop had on his calendar meetings with the diocesan finance board in the morning and the Board of Consultors in the afternoon. I knew that I would not see him until it was time for our driver Fred to take us back to the official residence of the bishop of Wallington. Bishop William Harrington was the eleventh bishop or ordinary in the history of our diocese. The house had been given to the diocese during the time of our second bishop. So our present bishop was the eighth man to live in residence. Most of the former bishops did not have a priest secretary/master of ceremonies live with them. I was only the third priest to be so appointed. It was not a position a priest sought out or wanted. You are isolated when living with the bishop. Most of your priest friends and classmates really are uncomfortable just dropping over to visit me. No matter how pastoral a bishop is, he is still the person who can transfer any of us from one parish or assignment to another with or without our consent. We all promised the bishop who ordained us "obedience and respect. To him and all of his successors." As the legitimate successor to Bishop Henry Pole, his predecessor of happy memory, who ordained us as priests, we owed Bishop Harrington our complete obedience and respect. Not all of my friends were men who approved of the changes Bishop had enacted since he arrived and felt uncomfortable being around him and especially in his residence. That is why I usually meet them at some neutral place or their rectory. In the first year as priest secretary to the bishop, I resented and was hurt by the way my friends now treated me. Now, after these number of years, I understand their distance had nothing to do with me, but rather their own unease and feelings toward the bishop. It just struck me, as I tell you this fact of life, that I am going to have to reexamine what they may have said to me about Bishop. Did any of my colleagues ever threaten him in the past? Did they ever "joke" with me how they could kill him over the latest change or regulation he had made for the diocese? I was sure Detective Teeling would be asking that question of me tomorrow.

I spent the rest of the evening in my study thinking about the last few years and who may have, even jokingly at the time, threatened our bishop. Honestly, for the life of me, I do not believe any of my colleagues would do such a thing, but at this stage, everyone was under suspicion. Next to my phone on the desk was a list of four names I had jotted down over the course of my trying to remember our many conversations. My gut told me it could not be one of the four. However, I was bound to turn them over to Jimmy Teeling at the cemetery meeting.

Saturday morning, after we had eaten breakfast, Sister Kunegunda, OC, brought my cleaned, folded, or ironed laundry to the room. It was such a blessing having her iron my white cuff link shirts every week. It saved a great deal on dry cleaning bills for sure. She hung the shirts up in my closet but left everything else on the bed. Sister never went into our dresser because she felt that was off limits. As a result, she would leave mine and Bishop's other clothing on the bed for us to personally put away.

I had made, as requested by Bishop, copies of the six letters he had received so that we could give them to Detective Teeling. He would guard the material against prying eyes, but at some point, I was sure, he would have to bring others into the case if he could not solve it by himself.

Bishop and I had a quick lunch of tomato soup, tuna sandwich, salad, and a cup of tea. We knew we would have to leave the residence by one thirty if we were to be on time for our meeting at the cemetery with Detective Teeling. After lunch, I went to my room to get the copies of the six letters that Bishop had received. When I got downstairs, I could see that Fred had already pulled the car up to the front entrance and was standing by the rear passenger door waiting for Bishop to come out and enter the vehicle. Punctual as always, Bishop was already coming down the front steps at one twenty-five.

I knew he was hoping that the extra few minutes would take care of any traffic issues, red lights we could possibly encounter as we went across the city to the cemetery. By now you know that one thing Bishop Harrington cannot stand is being late or being kept waiting. Today was no exception to that rule. Fortunately, there were no traffic jams, and we made it there about five minutes ahead of time. Fred stopped right in front of the small chapel on the property and got out and opened the door for the Boss.

When we entered the chapel, we were surprised to find Jimmy Teeling already there and waiting for us. Mind you, I did not see his usual black car outside and wondered how he had gotten here. He immediately got up from the chair he was sitting on and went over to Bishop, genuflected on his right knee, and kissed the bishop's ring. Virtually no one did that anymore, most just shake hands with the bishop. But Jimmy was third generation Irish Catholic men who had served on the same police force, and old habits of respect did not die quickly with them. Bishop did not try and stop Jimmy from kissing his ring (I actually think he enjoyed it) and said how glad he was to see the detective again. The last time had been just two months ago at the Police Associations Annual Fundraiser, and Harrington had been invited as one of the speakers. After I shook Jimmy's hand, no time was wasted. Immediately Detective James Teeling asked Bishop when the first letter arrived and why he had not called the department about it. I knew Bishop was uncomfortable being questioned about his judgment regarding handing these letters over. I cut in and said to Jimmy, "The issue was not when he should have alerted you, but the fact that we have and need the advice to move ahead on this."

Jimmy did not like my interruption, nor my dismissal of his pointed question to the bishop.

Bishop now spoke directly to our detective and said he had not because, at first, he thought it was a prank letter from some disgruntled person. As the letters continued to come, once a month for six months, he realized this person was not only dangerous but probably was going to attempt to carry out the threat. Bishop did not want anyone to get hurt. He said he was personally not afraid to die, but if this person did it at one of the many functions, ceremonies he attended, innocent people would probably be hurt as well. What he wanted to know was if it possible for the diocese to handle this. Immediately, Detective Teeling said there was no way it can. There were things we could do, but as far as getting to this person he did not believe it possible. He then asked to see each of the letters in the order that Bishop had received them.

I handed the file over and told him all six were in there, and to the best of my knowledge, they were in the order that Bishop had received them. Jimmy laid the six of them out on the altar of the chapel next to one another. The person had used a different print style each time they sent the letter. The first ones were more generic in nature and their complaint. However, all of them ended the same way, telling him that he was going to die. I arranged them on the altar in the order Bishop had received them so Detective Teeling could look at them all.

Letter One, January

Your Excellency,

You preach about helping the poor, homeless, weak, and the old. Yet you ride around in your chauffeur-driven vehicle, with your boy-toy at your side. You live in your mansion with him, and I never read about you taking in a homeless person, personally feeding the poor, or taking someone out of a shelter and giving them a job. No, you just want us to do what you do not. You are a phony, a real fraud, and should die.

Letter Two: February

Your Bishopness,

I see you ignored my last letter. Your lifestyle has not changed. Yet yesterday you asked the people of the diocese to donate or pledge fifteen million dollars so the diocese could continue its good work. What a laugh, you hypocrite!

Did Jesus EVER ask his followers for money? Did Jesus ever dress in expensive clothing and meet with other expensively dressed people and ask them to dig deep into their pockets to support your work? I only remember him driving men like you out of the temple. You are a fake of the first class, a sinner, and you shall die.

Letter Three: March

Bishop W.

You choose to ignore me. But then I am not one of the people who are willing to "kiss your ass" to have you speak or show up for an event or ceremony they are having.

Why do parishes pay you, or as I understand you like to say, "gift you" with money to confirm their young people? It is your job as bishop to confirm. You should not be looking for an envelope to be given to you with money for doing your damn job. For that alone, you deserve to die, and you shall be in the very near future.

Letter Four: April

Hey, blind fool!

You think you're smart doing nothing to change your and the diocese's way of doing business? That is going to stop with your untimely death.

Over the last thirty years, all we have read about or seen on our TV screens are the endless sins of the Church. It launders its money through the Vatican offices, priests embezzle money from their parishes, abuse kids, have mistresses, take lavish trips, drink like skunks, and abuse drugs. What do you do? Virtually nothing in the years you have been here. Oh yes, you may have penalized a priest or two, but you allow the others to continue with their women whores, take Church funds, and really abuse drugs and alcohol. Your days are now shorter, and you better start your prayers for forgiveness.

Letter Five: May

Hey, fancy pants in your regal robes. Enjoy them while you can because you will not be wearing them much longer. The only ones you will keep are the ones they bury you in.

You can be sure that I will not be kissing your ring or ass, but putting a bullet through your evil heart. The clock is ticking, and it is almost midnight.

Letter Six: June

I have wasted too much time with you and your poor leadership. Judgment Day is upon you, Harrington.

The church and this diocese are corrupted to the core. The last face you will see is my smiling face as I put you to death.

My next communication with you will be my last and bring you into hell.

Detective Teeling stared at the six letters and looked up at Bishop Harrington and told him that this was not good. Not only should he and the diocese be taking this person seriously, but he should start to protect himself and those around him. Teeling told Bishop he was sure that the chief would okay an Officer to guard the residence. Bishop instantly refused and said he would not agree to taxpayer money being wasted on him. Detective Jimmy reminded the bishop that he was also a public figure and head of this diocese. He then insisted that tomorrow, Bishop starts wearing a bulletproof vest under this clerical front and suit jacket. He did not believe the killer would be expecting that, and it might be the very thing that saved Bishop's life. Bishop began to open his mouth in protest, but this time, Jimmy cut him off. He looked Bishop in the eye and told him that he had asked for his advice and now he was giving it. Plus, as a Catholic himself, he had a vested interest in keeping the bishop of his Church alive and would not take no for an answer. Since none of us ever speak to him that way I know Bishop was totally caught off guard. All he could manage was a definite shaking of his head. Detective Teeling smiled and said now the real work of policing could begin.

Detective Lieutenant Teeling would honor the request for the department being discreet in its handling of this matter. Our detective friend told Bishop Harrington that four other detectives under his command also were active Catholics in this diocese. He knew that once they saw these letters, they would all do whatever it took to make sure that no harm came to him if it was at all avoidable. There would be no press release, no leaking of information, but Bishop had to do what he was asked; otherwise, they could not do their respective job. Bishop stood there, quiet for a minute or two mulling over what had just been said. Finally, he said he would do what he was asked if it did not interfere with his commitments or his schedule of parish visits and Confirmations. Since Detective Teeling had gotten that concession out of Bishop, he was not going to press his luck and ask for more at this time. He simply genuflected, kissed Bishop's ring, and assured him he would do all that he could to bring this to an end as quickly as possible. Jimmy then left the chapel, and there the two of us stood. Finally, Bishop said he thought it was the time that we also went back to the residence and reexamine his schedule to see if there was anything that could be dropped or rescheduled for a later date.

When we come out of the cemetery chapel, Fred already had the car door open for Bishop to get in. When we were both in our seats, Fred started up the engine and brought us back to the house. That evening, our housekeeper, Sr. Kunegunda, OC, informed Bishop that there was a man from the police who wanted to see him. Bishop Harrington went down to greet this unexpected visitor. He introduced himself as Detective Sergeant Williams. He quickly told Bishop that Chief Teeling had sent him over to fit Bishop with a bulletproof vest. He had three different-sized ones with him in the car. Det. Williams measured Bishop and said he would be right back in. He came in with the jacket, showed Bishop how to properly attach the straps, and reminded him that he agreed to wear it whenever he left the residence. Bishop asked him if he was one of the four who Detective Lieutenant James Teeling said would be working with him. Detective Williams assured Bishop that he was and that he was a member of St. Cecelia Parish. Bishop thanked him for bringing over the vest, serving the community and being an active member of St. Cecelia Parish. The detective shook Bishop's hand and told him, like the others, he would do all in his power to protect and get into custody whoever was making these threats.

Bishop came upstairs and down to my rooms, knocked on the door, and when I opened it, he showed me the vest and said it was not as thick as he thought it would be but not nearly could you consider it comfortable to wear. I reminded him that he had agreed to wear it. The Boss assured me that he told Detective Sergeant Williams that he would. The name did not ring a bell of recognition in my head. He was either a relatively young detective or possibly someone the Force had hired from some other department to beef up the Criminal Investigation Division (CID) that Jimmy was head of with the rank of detective lieutenant, although everyone called him chief of detectives.

Sunday morning, Bishop was celebrating Mass at the parish of St. Helena. As usual, I would be going with him as master of ceremonies. St. Helena was one of our suburban parishes with about six hundred registered families. It still operated a Catholic elementary school from pre-K through eighth grade. I believe they had just under five hundred students in attendance this year. In this time of closing, schools and parishes, because of a lack of active participation, it is a real blessing to find a school and church doing so nicely. I knew that Bishop was looking forward to celebrating the ten o'clock Eucharistic Liturgy with the people and spending time after the Liturgy greeting them.

I had everything packed that we would need, namely, his miter and crozier, the gloves and over-the-shoulder shawls with his crest imprinted on them, and that the two servers would wear who are charged with holding his miter and crozier when he was not using them.

We arrived at the parish around 9:30 AM, which gave Bishop time to spend a little time with the priests assigned to the parish, as well as those helping out. At nine fifty, Bishop took off his suit jacket to put on his alb, and I noticed the bulletproof vest outline under his white cuff link shirt. I did not say anything and just helped him slip his alb on, cincture, stole, and chasuble. I then put on him his pectoral cross over the chasuble, miter on his head, and crozier in his left hand. Bishop carries it in his left hand, as all bishops do, is so he can bless the people with their right hand. It also frees that hand for him to greet parishioners with when the Liturgy is over.

The church was at capacity, the choir sang marvelously, and the people seemed interested in the homily of Bishop Harrington. He even had the little children laughing in their places when he mentioned characters from Sesame Street. Even I was shocked that Bishop knew their names and what role they played. Even after five years going around with Bishop, he still surprises me.

After the Liturgy, he went back to the rectory, took off the wet clothing, put dry ones on, and once again spent time with those who were counting the day's collections, the housekeeper, and cook of the parish.

We went back to the residence at around eleven fifty and were right on time for lunch when Sr. Anesia, OC, rang the dinner bell.

On the drive back, I did say that I noticed the outline of the vest under his shirt and was happy he followed the instructions of Lieutenant Detective Teeling. He just looked at me and nodded.

Chapter 3

Most of this new week was business as usual. Bishop had a series of meetings that were scheduled for here at the chancery. We did not have any community or parish events to attend. I knew that the Boss would be spending much of his time getting ready for the National Conference of Bishops' meeting that will be held next week. He already had his flight booked but needed to go over all the material that was scheduled to be discussed at this meeting. For this session, he will be traveling alone. Only the bishops of the United States attend the daily sessions. All have a right to speak and vote on the main issues or statements that will be released by the Conference.

Previous to this week, I had gone over the materials Bishop Harrington had been sent for the Conference and made notations where I thought he might want to ask for clarification or speak up on the subject. Bishop was a strong believer in preparation, study, and prayer before one opened their mouth at a regional conference of fellow bishops.

I forget to mention that on Tuesday of this week gone bye, Detective Teeling called me to let me know that the six letters we received had been printed out on different printers. Through careful analysis, they had determined that they were not done with commercial printers that many stores have available to the public. Those have a distinctive style to them and are traceable. Moreover, had this person used one the machines, the memory chip would have a copy of the letter on it and the day and time it was produced. That would have led to the team asking to see the stores video of that day and time. Unfortunately, our person did not use a public machine, which means they had access to six different devices. Either they owned a lot of printers or possibly had accomplices who know of their intent to kill the bishop. The department would have to consider that and the reality it may not be alone individual that is involved.

Naturally, anyone hearing news like the above would not be overjoyed. I asked Detective Teeling if I should relay to the bishop that there could be more than one person involved. Jimmy asked for now that I do not inform him. It would not change how he went about business, and he had enough on his plate as it was without worrying about a conspiracy to murder him. I agreed that at this stage, it would be best that it just be between us. However, it did make me wonder how much danger Bishop was really in.

On Saturday afternoon, Bishop was scheduled to celebrate the Eucharistic Liturgy and Confirm seventy young men and women at St. Michael's Parish. It was one of our rural parishes, and you are probably wondering how they could have seventy being Confirmed if not a city church. Legitimate question for sure, and the answer is simple. Four of our rural parishes have teamed up and prepared the young adults for the sacrament. They agreed that each would share resources, personnel, and the preparation classes would move from one parish to the other. In the end, all of them would bring their young people to the church designated for that year and have them Confirmed. This year, it happened to be St. Michael's Parish that is the host to the other three for this celebration.

At the end of the Liturgy, Bishop processed out, crozier in his left hand and blessing the people in the pews as he went down the aisle. As he went out the front doors of the Church, a single shot was heard, I saw the crozier spin and fall to the ground. Bishop staggered and reached out for the door to support himself and slid to the ground. My heart stopped beating, or so it seemed, and I ran to him.

He looked dazed, scared, and his face was very pale as if all the blood had rushed out of it. I could not see any blood, but with his vestments on, it was not clear where the bullet had entered. I lifted up the chasuble, the outer garment, and did not see blood. One of the ushers had already called 911, and the police and ambulance were on their way. The pastor and the three other pastors gathered around Bishop and decided that they would move him to the rectory and out of view. I went to pick up his metal crozier and realized what had happened. When Bishop walks, the crozier bends forward, and apparently, when the shooter took their shot, his crozier moved in front of the bullet and deflected it. There was a dent in the thick metal where the bullet had hit and bounced off. If the sun had not forced Bishop to shield his eyes and pull up on the crozier at the exact moment, the bullet would have surely killed him on the spot.

The police arrived and ambulance crew who methodically checked Bishop out. They confirmed that the bullet had not hit him, but that his blood pressure was very high and wanted to take him to the hospital. He said no; he would go with the pastors over to the rectory and recover there. I showed the officers his crozier and where the bullet had hit. They said they would take it and have it analyzed as to the type of bullet. Naturally, they would be carefully checking the grounds to see if they could recover it.

All Bishop Harrington could tell the police was that as he came out the opened church doors, the sun made his eyes squint, and at that moment, this crozier spun in his hand and flew out of it. He heard the single shot and was sure it was aimed at him. Bishop Harrington no sooner had finished giving the officer who arrived his statement when our chief of detectives burst into the rectory like a bull in a china shop. James wanted to know if Bishop was all right and if he had done what he was asked to do (wear his vest) and if he saw anything. Bishop patiently told him the same thing he told the first police officer. Then, Bishop asked for me and if it would be okay for him to get out of these vestments and sweaty clothing. Detective Telling said he had no objection and the pastor of St. Michael's led us to his suite of rooms so Bishop could change.

The first thing he did was plop down on the bed. He looked at me and said, "John, I am not sure my legs are going to hold me upright now, you are going to have to really give me a hand changing today."

I told him I would handle it all. So I removed his pectoral cross first then his chasuble and stole. I helped him up so I could release the cincture around his waist and remove his alb. Bishop sat down again. I knew all his dry clothing was in the small suitcase he always had with him. I opened it and found new underwear, collarless white cuff link shirt, and clerical frontal with attached collar. I took off his present clerical front, white shirt, and undershirt. They were soaking wet with perspiration. As I started to roll them up to put them in the suitcase, he snapped at me and told me not to roll the clerical front but to fold it neatly, so it did not get wrinkles. He did not want to incur the wrath of Sr. Kunegunda over it when we got home. The Boss had never snapped at me before, so I knew the stress was getting to him. Gently I folded the clerical front and laid it on top of the shirt and undershirt that I had rolled and put in a plastic bag. When I was able to dry him off, get the undershirt and new clerical shirt and frontal on, I watched him slowly push himself off the bed and stand. For the first time that I have known him, Bishop looked his age and probably five years added as a result of today's event.

When we reentered the room where the priests, police were gathered, Bishop asked if it would be all right if he just went home instead of spending time with them as is his usual practice. Needless to say, everyone agreed that he should get back to the residence. Detective Teeling told him that a patrol car would escort his car home. When he started to protest, Jimmy just looked at him with his best tough guy face, and Bishop finally shook his head okay. We excused ourselves and went outside where Fred McNamara had pulled the car right next to the side entrance. Bishop got in and so did I. Instantly, a patrol car pulled in front of our car, turned its lights on, and motioned for Fred to follow. We were home in no time as cars pulled over to the side when they saw the flashing lights in their mirror.

Upon entering the residence, Bishop went right up to his rooms. I carried the suitcase up and left it in his study. He told me he was going to go to our chapel to pray vespers and then get some sleep. Tomorrow afternoon, he had to catch the flight to Washington, DC, for the Bishops' Conference. I told him that I was sure the president of the Conference would excuse him after what happened today. Bishop assured me he did not intend calling Charles Cardinal Wolfgang and telling him about the attempt on his life or anything else for that matter.

I left his study and went back to my own room to get into something less formal. All I wanted was to put on my sweatpants and shirt, have a beer, and try and figure out what I could about what happened. I quickly stripped out of everything I had on and slipped my dark blue sweat outfit over my naked body and went into my study. Took a beer out of the small refrigerator I had in the study, turned the TV on, and sat down at my desk. All of a sudden, I saw a picture of Bishop Harrington on the screen. The announcer was telling his audience how someone had tried to kill the bishop but that his crozier had saved his life. If Bishop thought he could keep this quiet, there was no chance now. Naturally, the three major networks picked the story up and now every bishop in the country would know. That was the last thing William Harrington would want or desire.

We concelebrated Mass in our chapel the next morning, had a quick breakfast, and I took the list of stuff Bishop wanted to be done during the days he was going to be gone. I had told him over breakfast about the national news coverage of the attempt on his life. He was not happy about that development. It would bring with it endless questions, concern, and offer of prayers from his fellow bishops. In no way did he want to be the center of attention, but now he surely would be. Fred had the car ready, door open when Bishop stepped out the front door of the residence. He told me, "Take care, John, and if there is anything I need to know about the case, make sure you call me. If I am not in the room, leave a message with the front desk to have me call you." I assured him I would and that I would also call Jimmy Teeling to find out what new information he might have for us.

Shortly after he left, I got in my car and drove myself to the chancery. All the talk that morning was about the attempt on Bishop's life. Rose, his office secretary, was primarily concerned. I assured her that our bishop was fine after a night's sleep and on his way to attend the national meeting of the United States bishops. She hoped that the time away would give him some relief. The security firm that provided our one guard, as of this morning, had added another. Naturally, we would be billed for the additional man. The Vicar-General had agreed to the expense and thought it was a prudent move. The firm, for the most part, only hired retired police or recently discharged military police offers. Their training, background, and experience gave clients like ourselves a feeling that we were in good hands. I would go down and meet the new man when I went for lunch in our cafeteria.

No sooner had I reentered my small office then my phone rang. It was Detective Teeling. After a quick "Morning," he got right down to business. He informed me that the shot had come from behind a mausoleum in the cemetery across the street from St. Micheal's Parish. The team had traced the angle of the shot back to that place. It was an excellent place for the shooter. From the road or the front doors of the church building, you would not have a clear vision if you were looking over at the cemetery. The mausoleum was one of those that was built to hold four individuals. Plus, it had these two massive pillars on the outside corners of the building. It was the perfect spot to take a shot from and not be seen. Jimmy told me that after the shot was taken, the shooter probably just ducked behind the crypt, waited for all the panicked action to take place, and then probably just walked off. Whoever it was, they were good. They made sure they had covered their shoes with those paper booties, so there were no footprints and had picked up the spent casing. All the police were able to find was the bullet that had bounced off of Harrington's crozier. It was inside one of the evergreen bushes on the left side of the entrance. The shell provided some information to the squad. He would bring a report over to me tomorrow. He also asked that I informed him when Bishop was safely in his room at the hotel. I assured him that when Bishop Harrington called me, I would let him know.

The very next call that came through to me was from Cardinal Wolfgang asking me what flight Wally was on and what time was it due to arrive. I quickly looked at the copy of his flight schedule there and back and told the Cardinal that he was expected to arrive at 2:45 PM. The Cardinal thanked me and hung up. Cardinals do not spend time chatting with secretaries to the bishop.

Cardinal Wolfgang called the concierge of the hotel and told her that he wanted a limo to take him to the airport. He would pick his friend Wally up and make sure he arrived safely at the meeting. Cardinal Wolfgang then called his friend the Cardinal of Washington, DC, and asked him if he could get the necessary clearances for the limo to meet Bishop Harrington on the tarmac. He assured his brother cardinal that he would make the calls and see if it could be done. Thirty minutes later, he informed Cardinal Wolfgang that the driver was to go to gate twelve, there they would need to show ID but would be escorted from the gate to where the plane was to taxi to after landing. The pilots would be informed to have the flight attendants have Bishop Harrington remain on the aircraft and then a stairwell would be moved to the rear door of the plane for him to exit. Cardinal McCormick said he would be there as well as the mayor who insisted on being present.

And so it happened just as planned. The limo was stopped, credentials checked, airport police escort to the landing area where the mayor and Cardinal McCormick were already present. Cardinal Wolfgang got out of the limo and joined them. Just then, the plane hit the runway and began to taxi to the gate. Everyone deboarded the plane, except one, Bishop William Harrington. Then the rear emergency door of the plane opened to the stairs that had been brought up on the aircraft. A female flight attendant appeared pushing the door completely open, and then Bishop appeared. He shook hands with the flight attendant, descended the stairs to be greeted by his friends Charlie Wolfgang and Teddy McCormick. The mayor welcomed him to the city and assured him that while he was in DC, he and the other bishops would be safe and secure. She had ordered extra police to patrol outside the hotel and additional undercover officers to be in the hotel. Bishop Harrington was embarrassed by all the attention and told them all he did not believe anyone was in danger, that the threats had been targeted at him. He thanked the mayor and Cardinal Wolfgang for their concern for his welfare. They had known one another since their seminary days and were friends who did not see enough of each other. They then all got in the limo, and a police escort led them back to the hotel. They had assured Bishop that his luggage would be delivered to his room. Naturally, the conversation in the car was all about the shooting, the letters, and if he was okay. Wally assured his two friends that he had been shaken by the experience, had not really time to process the whole thing, but he thought he was all right. At least physically he was. Wally laughed and told them he would have to purchase a new crozier since his was now indented and bent from the bullet hitting it and in police custody. He then allowed them to pat his chest and feel the bulletproof vest he was wearing. If nothing else, our bishop was a man of his word. If he told you he would do something, like telling Detective Teeling, he would wear the vest when out and about, he did it.

The press was waiting at the hotel as the police escort, and limo arrived. The two Cardinals and Bishop stepped out from the vehicle as police officers cleared the way for them to enter through a barrage of questions from reports. Inside the hotel, staff greeted them, handed Bishop Harrington his room card, and the three took the first elevator up to his room. Not a suite of rooms, as was afforded to Cardinals in attendance, just an ordinary room with a queen-sized bed, small sitting area, bath, and open closet. Once ensconced in the room, his two friends left him and told him to get some rest before the opening session at seven thirty that evening.

Since Bishop did not have his suitcase yet, he sat down and called my cell number. As soon as I saw his name appear, I answered and asked him how his flight was. That led to a tale of complete embarrassment for him. He wondered how Cardinal Wolfgang knew he would be on that flight. I had to tell him it was me who told him, but what was I supposed to do when a Cardinal calls—ignore him, or say I don't know? Bishop said he had just not expected such commotion about his arrival or the attempt on his life. I assured him that everyone was concerned here at the chancery, and I was sure among our Catholic laity of the diocese. Bishop Harrington told me he was going to catch a short nap before he ordered room service for his evening meal. He thought it would cause less fuss if he ate in his room than in one of the hotel's restaurants. I told him that he should just try and enjoy the respite of being away, spending time with his bishop friends and let us back home take care of his safety. He laughed and told he would try, but no guarantee.

I cleaned off my desk, locked the office up, and went to leave the building and go home. I had driven to work since Fred McNamara only drives when Bishop is present and in the car. When I arrived at the entrance and reception desk, I noticed a new uniformed officer standing there. Then I recalled how the security firm was sending an additional man to assist our regular guard. I went over and introduced myself to him as Bishop's priest secretary and master of ceremonies. He told me his name was Bill O'Neil, and he would be assisting until this affair was cleared up, as he put it. I thanked him and assured him the next few days should be quiet since the bishop was in Washington, DC. He said I might be right unless someone wanted to check the building out, where the different offices were and all the escape doors. I just looked at him in astonishment. It had never crossed my mind that the person or persons would come into this building in an attempt to kill the Boss. We had people coming and going all day. Most of the major departments of the diocese were housed here. From the school office to the Office of Cemeteries and everything in between was housed on one of the three floors and basement of the building. Bill O'Neil then told me that for the foreseeable time, all visitors would have to show photo ID and a copy of it would be made before they were allowed into the main part of the building. A cold chill ran down my back at the realization of the danger we were all in and how close to home this now was for us.

Bishop Harrington, being away meant it was very quiet here in the residence. I did invite Father Lou Santiago over for dinner one night while the Boss was away. I knew that if he did not run into the bishop, he would accept, which he did. It was good for me to have a close friend like Louis to vent with, knowing that whatever I shared with him stayed with him. Sister Anesia, OC, had prepared a great meal of roasted chicken, mashed potatoes, homemade gravy, string beans, and hot biscuits. We must have spent forty-five minutes eating, laughing, and just enjoying each other's company. Sister brought out her famous apple crisp with vanilla ice cream on top for dessert. That and a good cup of coffee finished a perfect meal. Lou stayed till about nine thirty and said he had to get back to his rectory since he was scheduled for the 6:30 AM Eucharistic Liturgy tomorrow morning and still had to finish his homily. He always preached, even if it was only for five minutes, at the morning Liturgy.

I think I forgot to tell you what was in Detective Teeling's report. He had brought it over himself rather than send it by fax. The bullet shell they found in the evergreen bush was a 12.7 Nato round. Probably fired from 150 meters away, just about the distance the mausoleum was located. It was fired from a Dragunov sniper rifle, a Russian-made weapon. Whoever this individual is, it can now be presumed they are well trained and have had military training. The fact that he or she wore paper booties made sure they picked up the casing all showed signs of a person who knows what we would be looking for in the investigation. If Bishop Harrington had not pulled that crozier in front of him at the exact second he did, we would be at his funeral instead of looking over this report. The force of the shell had gone through the thick metal, spun it around and out of Bishop's hand before landing in the bush instead of his chest. Jimmy Teeling and his select group of detectives were leaning toward a group of individuals being led by one angry person.

The six letters were as he previously told us printed out on different printers. The paper was the same in all six of them. There were no fingerprints on the originals besides Bishop's and mine. Once the investigation got started in earnest, Detective Teeling had asked for the original letters so they could check for fingerprints. He had also asked for the envelopes, but Bishop had destroyed them and just keep the letters in his office at the residency. I was asked to supply them with all scheduled events that Bishop would be attending over the next four weeks.

I called Rose on the intercom and asked her if any new ones had been added that I did not have on my copy of his calendar. She assured me that there had been a few chancery office meetings that had been changed to different days or times, but that none of his outside commitments had been moved or cancelled. I went and printed my copy of his schedule outside the chancery office.

Chief of Detectives Teeling asked me if Mr. McNamara would be driving Bishop to all these events and how long had he worked for Bishop. I assured him that Fred was a dedicated and loyal employee of the diocese and that for twenty-two years, he had been the official driver of the bishop of the diocese, whoever that person would be. Jimmy looked at me and said that everyone was a suspect until deemed otherwise. I looked shocked and bewildered by that statement. Right off, I asked him if I was a suspect as well. He assured me that I had already been cleared by the detective charged with looking into the background of all who knew where Bishop would be at any given time. Does that mean Rose, the Vicar-General and chancellor are all considered suspects also? He looked back at me and only said, "Until cleared everyone is a suspect. Also, the four priest names you gave me have been cleared." I felt sick to my stomach. Not only is our bishop in danger, but that we could be thought as possible suspects were beyond anything I would have considered. I thanked Detective Teeling and asked that he keep me informed of any further developments.

That evening, I called Bishop Harrington at his hotel and told him what I had learned from Lieutenant Detective Teeling. Bishop was shocked to think it could involve more than one person.

I asked how the sessions were going, and he told me that they were to vote tomorrow on a national statement on immigration. Otherwise, much of the meeting had been going over and finishing work they had begun earlier in the year. The Boss asked me to give fair warning to Fred that there could be press waiting for him to come out the doors from the baggage area. He told me that he would call Fred by cell phone when he was getting ready to go outside so that the car could be already at the pick-up zone for arriving flights. Bishop did not want Fred getting out of the car to open the door, he would do that so they could get right back onto the road and on their way home. I assured him that I would take care of it.

Around four thirty the next day, Bishop Harrington was back at the official residence. It was good having him in the house again. Although we did not spend lots of time with one another on the nights we were home, it was still a comfort knowing he was safely back in the house and just down the hall. Somehow, I felt that he probably had the same sense of security as I when he was here.

Sister Anesia, OC, had made a London broil, medium rare for us with baked potatoes, corn nuggets, tossed salad. We had a glass of Chardonnay with it and coffee with our dessert of freshly baked apple pie with a generous portion of whipped cream on top. Over dinner, I told him how I met our additional security guard and how they implemented a new policy to enter the building. He looked at me and asked if he would have to show photo ID when he entered. I assured him that would not be necessary, especially because his picture hung over the desk of the lobby receptionist.

Chapter 4

Bishop Harrington was eager to get back to working in the office and a routine schedule. I am not sure if I mentioned that on the last day of the Bishops' Conference, Charles Cardinal Wolfgang asked if Bishop Harrington would come up to the front of the hall. Naturally, the Boss did not like where this was going, and surprises are not his favorite thing.

As he approached the front of the hall, Cardinal McCormick came down from the dais and stood next to him. One of the hotel employees wheeled in a cart with a large wrapped package on top of it. Now, for sure, our bishop was nervous and not knowing what to expect. Cardinal Wolfgang told his friend Wally that all the bishops present had contributed toward this gift for him in light of recent events in our diocese. Charlie then asked Wally to open the package. Red in the face, Bishop Harrington obliged and inside the box was a new crozier virtually identical to the one that had taken the bullet and been destroyed and was in police custody. Cardinal Wolfgang and the other assembled members of the hierarchy of the Roman Catholic Church in the United States broke into applause at the stunned looked on our bishop's face.

Since Cardinal McCormick was the regional archbishop of our area, he reminded Bishop that typically his crozier or staff would be officially presented to him upon his taking over of a diocese. In this case, Teddy and the other bishops wanted to offer this replacement to him as a sign of their unity and brotherly bond as Shepherds of the Church. Cardinal Wolfgang asked that all the bishops pray with him and together bless this new crozier that hopefully, Bishop Harrington would get to use for many years. And so, without stretched hands, some two hundred plus bishops prayed over the crozier, asking God to bless all who Wally would be sent to shepherd and to protect him on his journey of leading the faithful to the Kingdom of God. Bishop was emotionally touched by the gesture of his fellow bishops and the gift they had given him. He thanked them for it and assured them that he had every intention of continuing to do his job. He would not cut back on his public schedule or not defend the faith that he swore to pass on faithfully to those under his care.

Almost all of the bishops, after the final prayers of this conference, were completed came up to

Wally and offered their prayers and full support to him. He thanked each and was immensely touched by their kindness and concern.

Now you know how Bishop, in the weeks to come, would be photographed with his crozier in hand as if nothing ever happened to it. There would be a lot of opportunities for pictures as we would be visiting all our secondary schools over the next few weeks. Each year Bishop went to each high school, celebrated. Mass with the student body and faculty and then had lunch with the faculty and staff. He did not intend not doing it this year. I personally believe these school Liturgies were not ones Bishop overly enjoyed. As an older man, in his late sixties, Bishop always wondered if he actually connected with the teenagers who sat before him as he preached. This year, it would be different, I was sure. Every student knew that someone had tried to kill Bishop. A few of our schools are situated in areas where our students live with street violence every day of their life. Bullets have been known to fly through their neighborhoods with innocent people caught in the crossfire or by drive-by shooters. Naturally, I would be going with him to all eight schools as his master of ceremonies.

Our first high school has about five hundred boys and girls in it and a faculty of fifty-three teachers, not counting the administration, which adds another four to the number. Bishop vested in the principal's office, and as we walked down the hallway toward the gymnasium where the faculty and students were gathered for the Eucharistic Liturgy, I could not help thinking what a striking image Bishop Harrington projected. Standing at six-foot-two tall, weighing two hundred pounds, perfectly white hair and black-rimmed glasses, he was a good-looking man. When I put his miter on, he now stood from toes to the top of the miter over seven-plus feet tall. We could hear the choir singing, music playing the entrance hymn. Local priests and pastors were concelebrating the Mass with Bishop and Father John who was the principal. As Bishop entered the gym, the last person in the procession, we were caught totally off guard. From the bleachers behind us, it started. Soon the whole student body and faculty were applauding Bishop as he entered their gym to celebrate Mass with them. The choir could no longer be heard over all the clapping. Bishop just smiled the whole way in and up onto the stage where the altar was set up. This was the first time, in all the years we had visited schools, that this has happened. He kissed the altar and took his place. The applause just keeps building until finally Bishop raised his hand and motioned for everyone to sit and for quiet. Slowly, and I mean slowly, the faculty and student body became quiet and found their seats. Bishop thanked them for their warm, hearty greeting. True to his calling, Bishop Harrington reminded them it was not so much him, but Jesus who they should applaud. It was his role as their bishop to lead them to Christ and the Kingdom of God. Then he asked them to stand and join him in the joyful celebration of the Eucharist.

During his homily, Bishop related how he had been shaken, scared at the time of the shooting. How he had allowed fear to virtually paralyze him at that moment. It was a concern Bishop told them that should not have existed. As a believer in the resurrection of the dead, and in the sacrificial death of Jesus for our sins, Bishop reminded the students that he should have not been so concerned about his life. What he should have been concerned about was whether or not he had led another generation to believe, to trust and place their lives in the hands of a God who loved them and called them His sons and daughters. The Boss told the students he had forgotten that at the moment his crozier was hit and he was ashamed of that fact. Bishop Harrington said he understood that many of them also feared for their lives. Bishop wanted them to know he truly related to that reality. Bishop then invited any student whoever started to doubt their belief, their value as a son or daughter of God, to feel free to contact him by letter or phone. He promised he would be there for them so they would know and have a sense of inner peace that only Christ can give us. I for one was moved by what he shared and wondered if any of them would take him up on his offer. Unknown to me, students did contact him by phone and letter. He invited them to join him at their school library to share what they felt, how could they believe when it was so hard and to have pizza with him. Fred drove him to the two sessions he had with the students and faculty members who wrote or called him. He did it all while I was away on vacation.

At the end of the Mass, as we left in procession the students sang the final hymn but also applauded for him until he was out of the gymnasium. When we got back to the principal's office, Bishop asked him to leave the two of us alone. I knew it was because he wanted to get out of clothing that would be sweaty and into a fresh set of things. After Bishop had changed, he invited Father John back into his own office and thanked him for the great Liturgy and reception. Father John told Bishop he had no idea they were going to do that and was equally sur-prised and proud of his students and faculty for doing it.

We did have lunch with the faculty and staff. The students had been released for the day after the Mass. Almost all the faculty and staff wanted to per-sonally come up and greet Bishop, and he obliged until the last person spoke to him. She was a female teacher in her ninth year at the school. Last year she had lost her second oldest to a shooting that took place on their street. He was walking his girlfriend to their house when the bullets started flying. Larry (her son) pushed his girlfriend to the ground, but before he could get down, one of the bullets hit him in the chest. He would die before his girlfriend and break open a mother's heart at the loss of a son. She just wanted Bishop to know she appreciated that he shared with the students his own fear, but also reminded them of salvation and hope in the Resurrection. It was all she had to hang onto and did in the weeks and months after Larry's death. Bishop gently hugged her and told her he would not forget her or Larry in his prayers. I knew that he meant every word he spoke to her.

Over the next six weeks, we would visit all our high schools. It was the two we had in the city that would be the only ones that greeted him with applause. I personally believe it was because they live with the reality of being killed much more than those of our students who live in the suburbs or rural areas of the diocese.

The weeks went by without further incident or letters. Bishop Harrington began to wonder if all the attention had made the person or persons give a second thought to the idea of his death. He asked me when the last time I spoke with Chief of Detectives James Teeling was. I told him it was about three weeks ago, and he had no new information to share with us.

On a lighter note, the new policy of photo IDs being shown when entering the building was comical the first couple of days. Employees who have worked here for years found themselves being stopped by the security guard and told they had to show ID. People looking through their pocketbooks, reaching for their wallets, all the while trying to explain they worked here and had for years. Two things came out of the new policy. The first was we had people late for work by the time they got cleared to go through to their offices. Second, we had to issue passes for all our employees so they could just show them and not have to have their photo ID available every day.

Rose, bishop's secretary, continued to carefully check anyone who requested a meeting with Bishop that he had not initiated. If she was not familiar with the name or person, she altered the Vicar-General or me. It was our job to check the person out before the meeting was set in his appointment book.

With the tension easing, I did get to go out with Father Lou to the movies twice and once out to our favorite Mexican restaurant. Louis always could make me laugh. His ability to tell stories, especially about his family, was hilarious. He was very close to his maternal grandmother who basically raised him, his brother and sister. Their father had left their mother when they were young children. Their grandparents became surrogate parents to the three of them. They all lived in their grandparents' home. To this day, Father Lou is still very close to his grandmother.

I do not have time or space here to begin telling you stories about his mom, sister, and older brother, or the extended family. If I did, you would be laughing so hard it would make it impossible for you to read on.

Let me just tell you one that frustrates Lou and is an utter amusement to the rest of us. He owns two small houses in his hometown in Mexico and a store with an efficiency apartment on the top floor. Every month, his beloved mother collects the rents. This has been going on for some twelve years. As of this writing, my friend, Father Louis, has zero money in his account. When he goes home to visit, he always questions his mother how it is possible that there is no money in the account. Every time, she pulls out a small book and shows him all the expenditures since he was last home. The problem for him is that all he sees on the page are squiggles. There is not a single legible number, name, anything understandable in the book. She will point to a section on the page and tell him this is where he loaned two thousand dollars to his brother's wife. Louis, in shock, tells his mother he never lent her money. The reality is that his mom is the one lending his money out to anyone who asks. In most cases, he never sees the loan repaid. The end result is that after twelve years he has from his four rentals amassed zero dollars for his retirement fund.

Every year in our diocese the Knights of Columbus have their annual Mass and luncheon with the bishop of the diocese. Not only do the Knights attend, but family and friends. This year, because the number attending has so increased they rented the city's outdoor stadium for the event. It seats about ten thousand when filled to capacity. The Knights only have reservations for about 6,300, but this stadium is still the only place that will accommodate the crowd. Generally, we would not give a second thought to celebrating the Liturgy in an open stadium. However, when I told Lieutenant Teeling about the use of the stadium, he was beside himself. Since his department was trying their best to keep the letters secret, he did not have the ability to call on the total force for such an event. He could imagine the shooter finding any number of places to hide and shoot from in that stadium.

Since the Knights had already paid the usage fee, sent out the publicity on the event, it was decided that the stadium had to be used. Jimmy informed the chief of police of how his men had been working on trying to solve who was behind the recent shooting and his concerns about the use of the stadium. The chief said he would okay additional personnel, especially the department's sharpshooters to be on duty that day. The rest would be left to us and our diligence in protecting Bishop Harrington at such public ceremonies.

When we were driving to the stadium, Bishop thanked me for my faithful service to him personally and to the diocese. It was the first time he ever said that to me and instantly made me realize he believed this might be our last ride together. I thanked him and assured my boss that everything that could be done was being done to protect him. Bishop just smiled at me and nodded his head. My eyes began to tear up with the realization that this indeed could be the last time we celebrated the Eucharistic Liturgy together.

It turned out to be a most beautiful day for an outdoor Mass. It was about seventy-six degrees with a gentle breeze. The sun was out, but not scorching or overbearing. Bishop dressed in his vestments and at the sound of the choir singing the procession of about sixty-two priests began. Fourth Degree Knights lead the way behind the cross bearer and two acolytes. They were dressed in full uniform, swords drawn and raised as Bishop passed through them toward the altar. The Mass went very smoothly. His homily revolved around the need of family and service. Not one of his best, but it was okay, and I did not believe the gathered faithful would be complaining.

Since the crowd of just about 6,150 people was too large to come down to receive the Body and Blood of our Savior, Jesus, twenty-five additional priests went into the bleachers and around the main entrances. Bishop and the Vicar-General distributed Communion in front of the altar. I could see the sharpshooters scanning the crowd and those moving toward the priests distributing Communion. The two acolytes, one next to Bishop and the other next to the Vicar-General were armed police officers wearing a simple alb. We were almost done with the distribution when my eye caught a woman approaching the Vicar-General for Communion. All of a sudden, her folded hands moved quickly to the purse strung over her arm. A gun appeared, and before I could even yell, she pointed it at Bishop and fired. The bullet hit him right in the chest, and he dropped the plate of consecrated hosts and fell to the ground reaching for his heart. Two concelebrants ran and picked up the consecrated hosts from where Bishop had dropped them.

Then there was sheer screaming, people running toward bishop and the woman. She was thrown to the ground by one of the police officers who was acting as an acolyte and cuffed. The EMTs rushed to Bishop in the hope of stopping the bleeding and get him to the closest hospital. Over the PA system, you could hear announcements for everyone to remain in their seats, to calm down and to pray for Bishop Harrington. Bishop was put on a stretcher by the EMTs and wheeled off the stadium grounds. What the crowd did not know was that the bulletproof vest had done what it was designed to do, namely, absorb the shot and protect the wearer. Bishop would have a bruise where the bullet had impacted the vest on his chest. I cannot even begin to tell you how relieved I was that Bishop was again spared his life, this time by his vest. Detective Lieutenant James Teeling was at my side thanking Bishop for doing as he had asked in wearing the vest. He promised a new one would be delivered to the house tonight to replace this one.

It was quickly decided to announce to the crowd that Bishop was going to be okay and that the Vicar-General would conclude the Liturgy with them. The Knights who were acting as his honor guard were shaken to the core and felt they had failed in their duty.

The ambulance pulled out with lights on and siren blaring just in case we were begin watched and the woman was not acting alone. A few minutes after they left the area, Fred pulled Bishop's car up, and he and I got in. Fred used his knowledge of the city and roads to take us home in no time. Once inside the residence, Bishop was able to go to his room to change and rest. The two sisters met us at the door and were beside themselves in seeing Bishop home and safe. They had been watching the Mass on TV and were as shocked and fearful as all the faithful on what they had seen. But now Bishop was home and upstairs, and that was all that mattered. I knew even Sister Kunegunda, OC, would go out of her way to make sure Bishop knew how happy the two of them were that he was all right.

The woman who refused to give her name to the police was taken to headquarters, booked, and now was waiting to be questioned. She was still hand-cuffed when Detective Teeling entered the room.

Jimmy asked her if she wanted something to drink and she indicated the glass of water that sat on the table would be okay. He now asked her why she had shot Bishop Harrington. At that point, she looked Jimmy right in the eyes and told him she wanted her lawyer present and was not going to answer any of his goddamn questions without her attorney. By law, once she has invoked a lawyer being present, he could not ask her any more questions.

We would learn that her name was Sarah Mitchell, the wife of a prominent lawyer in the city. Why she tried to kill bishop, we would not hear from her today. What Jimmy did learn was that even though she failed, it would happen and their message would get out. She was a rather attractive woman with dark black hair, strands of gray mixed in, with clear, penetrating eyes. The next day, she was arraigned on an attempted murder charge, and bail was set at a half million dollars. By late afternoon, bond had been posted, and she was out free until her trial. When Teeling called and informed me of that, my heart sunk. Out and about, the woman who tried to kill my boss, and we could do nothing about it.

At Bishop's request, Sister Anesia had prepared a light meal for us that evening. She had an assortment of cold cuts, freshly baked bread, homemade German potato salad, coleslaw, and our favorite strawberry ice cream for dessert. Over the meal, I informed Bishop of what Jimmy had told me about Sarah Mitchell being released on bail. He just raised his eyebrows and said he would pray for her. Pray for her was the last thing I wanted to do, and here Bishop was gentle, in his unique way, reminding me that judgment and justice belonged to God. He would do what he was ordained to do, and that is praying for God's people and try and lead them to heaven.

After dinner, we went to our separate rooms. We had decided, over dinner, that we would pray evening prayer privately this evening in the privacy of our rooms.

I had no sooner gotten to my room, and the house phone rang. I picked it up, answered as I always do, "Bishop's residence, Father Writerson speaking, how may I help you?" Instantly, I was being told by Cardinal Wolfgang to put his friend Wally on the phone. I buzzed his room and told him who it was. He thanked me and said he would answer the house phone tonight for he feared we would be getting other calls for him. And so we did. I gave up counting after the sixteenth call. Most were short, as I was sure, his fellow bishops were just calling to show support and offer their continued prayers for his welfare and safety.

The next morning, Bishop Harrington looked tired and beyond his years. It seemed overnight that he had aged. His face was more drawn, I could have sworn his hair was whiter, not that you could really tell, it just looked whiter this morning. After breakfast, we were taken to the chancery office and went to our respective offices. I have no idea what his day was like, but if it was anything like mine, all work was put aside, and all we did was answer phone calls and chancery staff stopping in to see if Bishop was really okay. I assured all who stopped at my office that he was fine, just a little shaken by yesterday's event.

As promised, his new bulletproof vest had been delivered last evening, and Bishop was wearing it this morning when we left the house. He does not like having it on in the house since it makes the sisters and I nervous seeing him in it. We know it is for his safety, but we do not want to consider that here he would not be safe. So he does not get into it until the time we are ready to venture out of the house. Even when he walks through the manicured property and the vegetable and flower gardens, he now wears it. He promised Detective Teeling that he would, and as I told you, he is true to his word.

Chapter 5

I had suggested to Bishop that evening that we could possibly cut back on his schedule of liturgical celebrations throughout the diocese and that I knew the Vicar-General would be happy to do his part in going to them instead of Bishop having to expose himself so often. He looked at me and said, "It was St. Ignatius of Antioch who said that 'Wherever the bishop appears, there let the people be, even as wheresoever Christ Jesus is, there is the catholic church,' so, John, I do not intend cutting back on my liturgical celebrations. End of discussion and tell Monsignor Thomas, our beloved Vicar-General, unless I am ill and cannot attend he will not have to fill in for me."

One thing about Bishop Harrington is that you always knew where he stood on an issue. Whether you agreed or did not, he said what needed to be said. Priests especially did not like him being so blunt with them.

I personally found that if you wanted to communicate something that would be lengthy to verbally explain it was best to type it out and get it to him ahead of your meeting with Bishop. He always read all letters and communications that were sent to him. His memory for detail was excellent. He often amazed pastors when he would be checking their parish records of baptisms, marriages, deaths, and so on, how he could remember that these numbers were higher or lower since the last time he had visited and gone over the books. I, for one, forget stuff all the time and thus keep notes stuck all over the place to remind me. It was one of the things that made Harrington an excellent administrator and I just his assistant.

The holiday season was upon us. Thanksgiving was just around the corner, so to speak, and Christmas not far behind. However, you would think that Christmas was before Thanksgiving. Virtually every major store I went into, on my day off, has had Christmas displays out since October, some even before that. The Church will start a new liturgical year with the First Sunday of Advent.

All of this meant that Bishop Harrington's schedule was busier than usual. We finished all the high school masses about two weeks ago. Must say this year there was a different atmosphere in all of them when Bishop was there with the students. I guess, just knowing that twice attempts have been made on his life, the students could relate to that and were most attentive to everything he shared with them. Both knew what it is like to be disliked by someone that they could do you harm. Many of our students have experienced cyberbullying or in some cases personal at school. Our schools have strict policies against that, and the administrators have been swift to act. We also have open discussions about inclusion, discrimination, respect for one another as sons and daughters of God. The school masses this year would always be remembered by Bishop and hopefully all the young men and women.

We, I should say, Bishop, will be participating in an Ecumenical Thanksgiving Service to be held this year in the Episcopal Church. Each year the gathering is in a different church, synagogue, or mosque in the inner city. When you consider it is a combination of all the faiths, the turnout is never that great. I think the largest was after 9/11 in this country. We probably had over two thousand in attendance that fall. I would imagine there will be about three hundred this time around. It is really the only time of the year all the major faiths gather to pray and give thanks to God for what we have and still hope to realize in the year ahead.

Usually, during Advent, Bishop tries to celebrate the Eucharistic Liturgy in different parishes throughout the diocese. It has been his practice to celebrate at one of the Saturday evening Liturgies, and then the next day at another parish. Plus, he tries to attend at least one of the many Penance Service that will be held during the season and hear confessions with the other priests in attendance. Naturally, on Christmas, he will celebrate midnight Mass here at the cathedral, his parish church. Then on Christmas morning, he will go to the local county jail and celebrate Mass with the inmates and guards that wish to attend. He usually gets there about an hour ahead of schedule and will administer the Sacrament of Reconciliation to any of the prisoners or staff that wanted to go. Pope John XXIII was the first pope to ever go into a prison, and he only told the inmates it was because they could not come to him so he would come to them. Our bishop actually thought that was indeed what a bishop should be doing and has made it part of his ministry since the time he was ordained a bishop.

Just after the First Sunday of Advent, Bishop and I came home from the chancery one evening, and when he went through his mail, he saw an envelope with familiar writing on it. He did not say anything until that night when he asked that I come down to his study. He was sitting in one of the overstuffed chairs he loved and had an envelope in his hand. On his lap lay a letter opener. Bishop asked me to sit down, and I did. He then told me he believed that he had received an early Christmas greeting in today's mail. He wanted me present when he opened and read it. So there I sat as the silver blade of the letter opener cut through the top of the envelope. Just a single sheet of paper was there I noticed. He read it quietly and then handed it over to me. Bishop then put the envelope in a plastic baggie, and I knew who it was from. Sure enough, our mysterious writer was once again writing him.

Here is what was contained in this letter.

Hey, Harrington,

> You have been a real lucky man so far. Almost like a cat with nine lives. Let me assure you that nine lives you do not have. We missed killing you twice now but are planning to make sure the next time will succeed. Just wanted to wish you your last Merry Christmas. Enjoy what time you have left. Sarah Mitchell sends her greetings also.

I handed the letter back to the Boss, and he placed it in the baggie and told me to give both to Detective Leiutenant Teeling tomorrow. Then he showed me a brass plate that was engraved and read, "I think a bishop who doesn't give offence to anyone is probably not a good bishop." It was authored by James Thomson. Bishop had it always before him on the house desk to remind him that he would not be able to please everyone and still proclaim a gospel of radical conversion and salvation.

The next day, I turned the whole thing over to Officer Detective Teeling has sent over to pick it up for him. Now we would wait to see what the department could make of it all. The one thing I noted last evening was that it said "We" instead of "I" and stated that Sarah sent her greetings. No longer does it seem that we should be looking at one person doing all this.

I received a call in the early afternoon from Detective Williams who said they had the envelope checked for fingerprints and found one set belonging to Bishop (he had given them his shortly after we turned the first communications over to the Detective Bureau and a part of someone else). They still had not received any hits on it, so it seemed it was not someone already in the system. But they did want me to thank Bishop for bagging both envelope and letter. Again, the letter did not have any prints on it. We both had worn the white gloves we carry with us for ceremonies so I knew ours would not appear.

I thanked Sergeant Willimas for keeping us informed and told him I would pass the information onto Bishop. Since there really was not much to say him, I decided we could wait till we were home after work here in the chancery.

The day went quickly with routine work that we all do here at the chancery. Rose continues to keep a close eye on who asks to see Bishop and tells me if any of his outside engagements have a change in the original arrangements. The Vicar-General Monsignor Robert Thomas and I continue to meet once a week just to keep one another abreast of what is going on. Bob is really a super priest and great asset to the diocese. He has an excellent rapport with the priests of the diocese, and Bishop Harrington relies on him to smooth ruffled feathers all the time. Bob's sense of humor is famous, and he is often invited to speak at fundraisers and dinners knowing that he will have the gathering laughing in no time. Our Vicar-General always delivers on that count and in the process helps raise a lot of money for our diocese.

Next week, I am scheduled to go back to the major seminary where I taught Moral Theology and Preaching. The new rector has asked me to speak to the third and fourth-year seminarians about what to expect when they are ordained. He requested that I address the three most common moral/preaching issues they should prepare themselves to handle. I am looking forward to going back, spending time with my former colleagues on the faculty, and sharing with the present seminarians what I believe they should be prepared to handle upon Ordination to the Priesthood.

I invited Bishop to join my family for Thanksgiving Day meal. Otherwise, he will be here at the residence with the Sisters but eating alone. He thanked me and told me to tell my mom that he would be delighted to join us for the meal, although would not be staying long after since he had a pile of work to do. That part I knew was correct since I see him bring it home each evening. Generally, my day ends when the office closes unless we have an affair or ceremony to go to that night. Bishop Harringtons will go late into the evening reading reports, going over liturgical and diocesan policy issues that have come to his desk for his approval or rejection. Some of this he gets done at the office, but most of his day there is filled with appointments, so he brings a great deal of the work home with him. He will bring much of it back the next day with notations all over for Rose to incorporate into his official response.

We continued our schedule of events, both civic and religious over the next couple of weeks.

The Thanksgiving Ecumenical Service had a better turnout than I had predicted. The local rabbi was the principal speaker, and Rabbi Jerome

Katz was excellent. He spoke of simple things that remind us to be thankful, like a child's smile, the stories told by grandparents, the report that the cancer is in remission. Or that we can gather and worship in freedom, that we do not have to "walk ten miles to church or school" like our parents had to in all kind of weather (the church burst into laughter since we all have heard that line in our lives). The clergy that participated greeted people as they went into the church hall for holiday refreshments and to socialize. All in all, it was a really well-done service, followed by a very joyful gathering of faithful.

On Thanksgiving Day, after Bishop celebrated Mass at the cathedral, we went back to the residence and changed clothes. Both Bishop and I were going in civilian clothes to my mom's house. I drove us both over to our family home. My dad had died ten years before, so these gatherings were my mother's doing. I have only one other brother (we are twins) and one sister who is younger than us. She has two children of her own, and my brother has three. I knew the house would be filled with noise, laughter, and a natural ease that comes when the family is able to get together.

As soon as we opened the front door, you could smell the roasting turkey. Boy, did that smell good. I knew my sister was going to be giving our Mom Gertrude a hand in the kitchen and that is exactly where we found her. My mother's face broke into a great smile as she quickly wiped her hands on her apron and came over to greet Bishop. To my surprise, he planted a kiss on her cheek and thanked her for thinking of him and inviting him into the family. She turned a bright red color and thanked him for honoring our family with his presence. Then she grabbed me and told me to "give your mother a kiss."

My brother Victor, his wife Kathy, and my three nephews were the next to greet us as we entered the living room. The boys, Baron, Thomas, and Henry were getting so big and just full of boundless energy. I do not see them as much as I would like. Valerie's two daughters Tracy and Cindy rounded out the gang that approached us. It was clear that Tracy and Cindy and Victor's boys were not quite sure how to greet Bishop. I naturally received hugs and kisses from all five of them. Bishop instantly said "hi" to them and gave them a high-five greeting, which they giggled over and enthusiastically returned to him. It was going to be a good visit for all ages gathered at the family table.

We had a typical meal of roasted turkey, homemade dressing, mashed potatoes, glazed carrots, green beans, creamed cauliflower, cranberries, gravy, and hot rolls. After Bishop Harrington lead us in grace, everyone dug in and were relatively quiet as we all savored the flavors of the meal. Then the tradition of sharing with all at the table each was thankful for began. We went around the table, Mom leading off, and ending with Bishop. He told the family that he was personally grateful to be able to celebrate Thanksgiving in such a loving environment and thanked the whole family for making him feel right at home.

We had dessert later that evening. Then Bishop and I excused ourselves and said we had to get back. Mom started to protest, but I gave her that look that told her to let it go. I knew that Bishop had work back at the residence and I was his driver and guardian. So we said our thanks and good night to all and went back home. Another Thanksgiving in the books, and I wondered if it would be our last together?

The chancery was closed the Friday after Thanksgiving, so we had some free time for ourselves. Bishop told me to take the day off since he intended to just work in his study. I thanked him and went and called my classmate Lou and asked him if he was free. He said that he would be by early afternoon since he had a few things to do this morning. We agreed to meet up at one thirty that afternoon.

We spent a few hours at the athletic club that we both joined about two years ago. First, we engaged in a very lively game of handball, with yours truly winning. I had an advantage since it was the sport I received my college athletic letter in. My partner and I in college even made the state finals and came in second place. It was a first for our college having gotten that far in the state tournament, so we were heroes on campus. After the game, Lou and I hit the steam room and then the showers.

We left there and went out for a light dinner and just took the time to enjoy one another's company and deep friendship. I told Lou about Thanksgiving at our house, and he related all the events when his immediate and extended family gathered for their meal. Naturally, it would not be a Hispanic gathering without music, which was supplied by his nephews. He laughed how the younger generation had adopted the ways of the family and was not ashamed to be Hispanic. Since Lou was the only priest in the family, he held a special place on honor. He did not like the particular attention but knew it went with being a member of this family, and he would not be able to change how they saw him.

On Saturday and Sunday, Bishop went to local parishes to celebrate the start of Advent. I was there as his master of ceremonies. And so the new church year began. I prayed that Bishop and I would have much more to celebrate and that Detective Teeling and his team would solve who was trying to kill Bishop.

Chief of Detectives Teeling had this past week told me that they were having the FBI check the partial print that was found and had one of their profilers coming up with what type of persons would be involved and what they should be focusing on at this stage of the case.

One of the local nursery owners delivered a seven-foot douglas fir to the residence as a gift for us this Christmas. I cut off the base of the tree, put it on the stand, added water, and the sisters took over from there. I assured them that I could put the lights on, but they said the two of us had enough to do. And so, in between cooking, cleaning, and taking care of us, they put the lights on and all the ornaments. It looked great when it was finished.

I knew it would not be complete until the manger scene had been set up. As members of the Order of the Cross, the sisters made sure all the figures were in their correct place. Shepherds and sheep off to one side, Magi traveling to the site from the east, and in the stable, Joseph, Mary, their donkey, a cow, and a mouse. Yes, a mouse. The sisters insisted how you could have an outdoor manger with hay/straw in it and not have mice? I am sure St. Francis of Assisi who created the first Creech had never thought of that. They did not believe the figure of the baby Jesus should be in there until Christmas day. They wanted Bishop to add him after we came back from the Midnight Celebration of the Birth of Christ. I also knew that both sisters would be up and waiting for us when we came home so they could see Bishop bless the scene and place the infant in front of Mary and Joseph.

I don't know if I told you that both sisters live here with us. The residence, when it was built, had a section for servants' quarters. The original owner had a cook, housekeeper, two serving servants, plus the carriage driver. Both sisters are probably in their seventies but being in full habit, I am really not sure. They wear a white habit, red cincture with a dark red tunic over it, and a white cowl attached to the red tunic. On the front of the tunic is a large gold-embroidered Jerusalem cross. The men of the Order wear the same outfit. When they are buried, the white cowl is pulled over their face just before burial. Bishop Harrington and I are blessed to have them here with us day in and day out.

Chapter 6

This is the week I go back to the seminary to speak with the third- and fourth-year students. I finally settled on some issues that I think they need to be prepared to address in the first years after their ordination to the priesthood. I did call the rector and bounced them off him to make sure it would not be overkill of material they have already studied. He agreed that he was almost certain that it was not, but he would check with the head of the Moral Theology Department to make sure. If I did not hear back within a day, it meant the topics were excellent.

When two days passed and I had not heard from the rector, I finished up my notes. I was sincerely looking forward to being back in the classroom and then in the evening with the faculty members that I taught with when assigned to the seminary.

I flew up to the seminary on Wednesday night and was met by Father Larry, the head of the Moral

Department and my former "boss." Larry always looks serious, even when he is joking around. He is also an excellent theologian and been teaching in the seminary for a good ten years. Bishops and religious order superiors are supposed to send their best to be seminary professors and Larry fit that bill. As we were driving from the airport to the seminary, we caught up with what we both had been doing since I left the school and became master of ceremonies and assistant to the bishop. Larry told me how pleased he was with the topics I chose because he did not believe these young men realized what they would be encountering when they were sent to parishes or schools of their respective dioceses.

The next day, I was to have one session in the morning and one in the early afternoon with the students. I had chosen to look at the questions/issues of geno editing or gene modification in babies while in their mother's womb. Second, I wanted to address the issue of same-sex couples and transgender members of their parish or school. Finally, I wanted to stress how important it was for them to live a simple life, immersed in the life of those they served. That was the keyword. They were ordained to serve the people of God and unless they grasped that they would never be the moral leaders the community needed. And so, from the clothes they purchased, to the cars they drove, all were a sign of either simplicity or privilege.

The two sessions with the students produced lively discussions, debate, and some fear from them. If they were to be a beacon that showed the way for others to avoid danger, then they would have to address these issues and so much more. I knew, having taught there, that academically they would be prepared. At least the professors would have done their best to prepare them. However, psychologically, emotionally, and spiritually those first two years are hard on a newly ordained. Much is expected of them from the moment they take up their assignment. I wanted to make sure I emphasized how important having a support network in place. Brother priests they could rely on and trust when they were feeling overwhelmed or lost. I told them it was not a sign of weakness to say that you didn't know what to do or say in certain situations. Those were the moments it was necessary to open up to another priest friend and share what they were feeling and experiencing.

The third- and fourth-year men were appreciative that I had been so blunt on topics they had not actually given much thought to before today. In that, I felt I had done the job the rector had invited me to do. In the evening, I had dinner with the present faculty, then cocktails, and shared stories for about two hours afterward. Since I had an early flight back to the diocese, I had to excuse myself and get some sleep.

Larry took me back to the airport and thanked me again for being so honest with the men and raising awareness of topics that could be explored after I was gone.

I arrived back at the chancery around twelve thirty and went right to my office. I buzzed Rose and told her that I was back so she could inform Bishop. Knowing that tomorrow and Sunday we would be out for Advent Liturgies, I made sure that the parishes would have sufficient servers and everything was in order at that end before the workday ended here at the chancery.

Bishop was delighted I was back and made sure he told me so as Fred drove us back to the residence. He had his pipe out and was smoking up a storm as he shared what he had been about. Naturally, he wanted to know if I did a good job back at the seminary. I assured him that I did not disgrace the diocese with my presentation and believed it had been of help to the students. He just smiled, pipe in the right corner of his mouth, and said, "I had no doubt, John, that you would be great, you are a born teacher." It was nice hearing that from Bishop Harrington. He is not known for compliments, and so it was nice knowing that he felt the way he did about me.

When we got back to the house, both sisters were there to greet us. They told me how delighted they were to have me back. I knew I was home, where I belonged. When ordained, we leave our biological family and relatives and go wherever we are sent by our bishop. Many priests never find that sense of warmth, of coming home, which I am fortunate enough to have here. So many rectories are cold places. Each man living alone or in their rooms only seeing one another at meals, if even then. It is not an easy life for many priests. Sometimes to fill that void, the sense of loneliness they experience a man will cross the line and engage in activities that are neither faithful to their commitment to celibacy but can be harmful or illegal. This diocese, like many throughout the country, has had its issues with priest alcoholics, drug dependent, depression, or sexually active. Bishop Harrington has not, since the day he arrived, every tried to cover up or hide misdoings by his priests. He has done all he could to implement the national policies of the Bishops' Conference but has shown remarkable compassion for every man or victim involved. The Boss has met with every single victim of sexual abuse and their families. He has had priests enter therapy for drug, alcohol addiction and made sure others could afford treatment for depression. Men who are sent to rehabilitation houses are never pleased with Bishop. Yet Bishop knows if he does not do it, then he failed them as one who is entrusted with their welfare and good health. Bishop's hope is that when their time is over at the rehabilitation center, they will have come to see how needed it was and be grateful he sent them.

The parish celebration of the Advent Eucharistic Liturgies went off very smoothly. The people genuinely seemed pleased to see that Bishop Harrington was okay and still continuing his ministry as bishop.

On Wednesday, Bishop celebrated Mass here in the chancery for all the staff. It is the first part of the annual Christmas office celebration that we share. After the Eucharistic Liturgy, the entire staff was treated to a catered meal. The finance office, at Bishops' direction, had hired an outside firm to handle the meal so our regular cafeteria staff would be able to join in today's Christmas celebration. Since Christmas falls on a Saturday this year, the chancery will close early on Friday. We do not exchange gifts officially, although I know some of the larger departments housed here do with a limit set on how much can be spent. The catering company did a great job of having a nice selection of hot and cold dishes available. Normally, we do not have this type of spread, but Bishop felt the staff had endured much over the last couple of months because of him. The tension of not knowing who was trying to kill the Boss, the new security procedure to get into the building, the added security had made many anxious. This was a way that he could personally thank them. At the luncheon, Bishop did just that. Reminding them all that the work they did was not for or about him. It was to assist the parishes of the diocese, to make the Gospel message known, and to be an example of fiscal responsibility and stewardship. After he had been finished sharing with them, everyone went back to their respective offices and the work they did.

I knew that I would be with him on Christmas night as we celebrated the Midnight Liturgy at the cathedral and the next day when he would celebrate Mass at the prison. Knowing that we would not finish till after the noon hour, I invited him to join my family for dinner. This time, Bishop declined. He thanked me for the offer, but he would have his meal at the residence. He had asked Sister Anesia, OC, to cook for four. Since she never questions him about who is coming to the house, she just said that would be okay. Unknown to me, Bishop had already invited Fred, our driver, to be one of the four. Fred lost his wife to cancer about four years ago, and Christmas is not one of his favorite holidays. Margaret, his late wife, was the one who decorated the whole house, baked endless cookies, and made sure we all got a box of them. Fred missed here a great deal. Bishop told me that he was going to ask Sister Kunegunda, OC, and Sister Anesia, OC, to be the other two at his table. He knew they would refuse, but he would insist. Bishop wanted his closest staff to gather with him and share a meal. When I heard of his plan,

I asked him if he would agree to one more being at the table. He looked at me strangely and asked who that would be. Looking him straight in the eyes, I said, "If you intend to have your closest staff with you, I want to be there." Right away, he asked what my mother would say. I told Bishop that once I told her the reason I would be having dinner at the residence, she would agree. He put his hand on my shoulder and said he would be delighted to have me there, and it was only because he knew I always went home that he had not invited me. That evening, he asked Sister Anesia if it was too late to add one more. She laughed and said there was always enough food and so one more at the table was not an issue. She would now set the table for five.

Bishop celebrated the Christmas masses without incident. After the midnight mass, we went back to the house, and Bishop blessed the manger scene and placed the figure of Jesus into the middle of it with Mary and Joseph overlooking their newborn child. Then he invited the two sisters to join him for the Christmas meal. As expected, they said that was not necessary and they would be fine. The bishop looked at the two of them and said, "Not even as a Christmas gift to me?" Both sisters burst into laughter and said it would be his gift. We all said "good night" and went to our respective rooms and beds to get a few hours of sleep.

On the way to the prison, Bishop asked if I would not mind hearing confessions with him this year. He reminded me that he fell behind schedule last Christmas because of the number of inmates and guards who wanted to go. The warden had not appreciated the significant change in the time set aside for guards and inmates to be at the Mass. I told him that it was not an issue for me.

When we had passed through the locked gates, had ourselves patted down, I immediately began setting out the things we would need. The prison chaplain was there and already had the altar arranged. Bishop told the guard in charge that besides himself and the chaplain that I would also be hearing confessions this year. The guard instructed one of the others to set out another two chairs, one for me and one for the penitent. We all put on stoles and took our places. The prisoners and guards started to come to us. Out of the thirty minutes that had been set aside for this, we used twenty-seven of those. I did not keep count, but the three of us heard a good number of confessions in that period of time.

One inmate provided guitar music of familiar Christmas carols, and the singing was enthusiastic with the rich tones of the male voice. It was a great celebration of faith and joy in a place where you do not always find either present.

Fred could tell that things went well by the quick step in Bishop's walk and that half smile of his. When we got back, Fred came in with us. After putting Fred in the main sitting room, where the tree and the manger were, I put on Christmas music. Bishop had gone up to his room to wipe down and change clothing. In no time at all, he was in the room with us.

I believe I mentioned before that we do not exchange gifts. However, as we were sitting there, Bishop pulled out two envelopes from his suit jacket and gave one to Fred and one to me. We both were shocked. Each of us received a Christmas card and inside a Visa gift card. I have no idea what Fred received, but mine was for three hundred dollars. To say I was speechless is an understatement. Fred and I both said, at virtually the same time, that we could not accept this gift. Bishop Harrington looked at the two of us and stated, "Not only will you take it, but that we should never forget how special we were in his life and in helping him do what he was charged to do as bishop."

Within moments of Bishop saying to us how special we were to him, Sister Anesia announced that our Christmas meal was ready to be served. The three of us went into the dining room and took our places at the table. Sister Kunegunda gave Sister Anesia a hand bringing everything out so that the two of them could sit down with us. Before we sat, Bishop prayed over the food, blessed it, and then asked us to sit. No sooner had we done that then he announced that he had something for the sisters as Christmas gifts. Both turned red and said that was not necessary and out of the ordinary. He just smiled and handed each of them a long envelope. Bishop asked them to open it. Inside were plane tickets for them to travel to their Motherhouse in South Carolina the last two weeks of January. Before they could say a word, Bishop told them that he had already spoken with Mother Veronica, OC, their Superior General and informed her of what he intended to do. She was most grateful to Bishop and assured him that places would be prepared for the sisters' visit. They were flabbergasted by this generous gift and his thoughtfulness. Before anyone could protest, Bishop said it was time to eat and enjoy the company of one another. Sister Anesia had outdone herself with the meal, and we did enjoy the time we had at the table. Stories of life were shared, of Christmas celebrations of the past and how lucky we were to be together this Christmas. Like myself, we all wondered if Bishop were doing all these things because he believed it would be his last with us. That was not going to be raised at this table. We all only savored the moment the five of us sat at the table for the first time in all these years. A time that would never be forgotten by any of us.

We all helped the sisters clear the table. Even Bishop joined in carrying dirty dishes to the kitchen and over to the dishwasher. We had a small industrial dishwasher, which would make cleaning up this mess an easier task. Fred thanked the sisters for an excellent meal and Bishop for inviting him to celebrate it with them. I, for my part, went up to my room, changed into civilian clothing, and told Bishop I was going to my mom's house and again thanked him for his generosity and the thoughtfulness of the whole Christmas celebration this year. Bishop thanked me for missing my mother's cooking and being with him, Fred, and the sisters. Whatever came over me, I do not know, but I just reached out and hugged Bishop. Not a word passed between us as I hugged him. When I let go, I do believe he was as surprised as I that I just did that. He then said, "I know, John, how much you care for me, I really do. Now get out of here and go to your mom." Tears ran down my face as I went down the stairs and out the front door.

Mom had already been to my sister Valliere's house to celebrate with her and the girls. Tomorrow she would spend the day with my brother and the boys. Tonight, it was to be just her and me. I told her about the gift from Bishop, his gift to the sisters, and what he said to me after I hugged him. Mom started to cry, and then I began to cry. Not of any sadness, just overwhelmed by his generosity and his kindness. My mother knew for sure now that I was in good hands living with Bishop. The two of us exchanged the gifts we had gotten for one another, and over coffee and apple pie with vanilla ice cream on top, we chatted the evening away. Just Mom and her oldest son (by some two minutes) in the comfort of one another. After my dad had died, she had relied on me to be the man of the house. Even being ordained, she still expected me to be there for her. Hopefully, the Book of Life will show that when it counted, I was there for her.

Chapter 7

Christmas was behind us and a new civil year had begun. It would be a special time for the diocese. This year, we would celebrate the 150th year of our founding as a diocese. It was not until late spring, but Bishop had already appointed the committee of priests and laity that would oversee the days of celebration. I knew they planned a concert the night before to be held in the cathedral. Invitations were going out this week to the bishops and cardinals, as well as the apostolic nuncio to attend. Bishop Harrington would send a handwritten letter to Pope James to attend. We know that he will not, but it is a protocol that he is invited. The Nuncio will express His Holiness's greetings and extend his blessing at the special Liturgy that would be held that Sunday. A large dinner would be held after the Eucharistic celebration, and all the bishops and civic leaders were being invited to attend.

Each parish of the diocese would be allowed to send ten parishioners to represent their church at the Cathedral Mass. Tickets for the concert the evening before were on a "first come, first served" basis. The choir would be made up of adults from all parts of the diocese. They began selection and practice last month. A young people's choir would also participate, made up of youth from all our elementary and secondary schools. Last I heard, it was a choir of 150 voices. I am sure it will be a night we will long remember.

My job will be to make sure we have sufficient vestments so that all concelebrants are dressed alike. Plus, there is the need to have sufficient vessels for the Communion of a group that large. Naturally, I will be working closely with the rector of the cathedral, Msgr. William Daley. Bill and I are longtime friends, and he is very easy to work with on things like this celebration. Bishop is officially the pastor of the cathedral parish, but as in all dioceses, a rector is appointed who handles the day to day operation of the cathedral parish.

Bishop and I also had to make plans for the two weeks the sisters would be away at their motherhouse visit. I knew that the cook from the rectory closest to our residence was making the first night's meal for the two of us. It would be lasagna. Bishop fell in love with Mary's lasagna dish about two or three years ago. It was after a Confirmation and the pastor at the time had invited many of the local priests to participate and stay for dinner afterward. One of the dishes that was served was the lasagna. I recall that Bishop had two portions of it and went into the kitchen and told the parish cook, Mary Jacoby, how much he loved it. From that time on, every time she made it for the rectory, she would walk over a small pan of it for Bishop and me. At first, I was not sure how Sister Anesia would feel about it, but she was most gracious in accepting it. Matter of fact, the two women became good friends. Each time Mary would bring a pan of it over, Sister Anesia insisted that she stay for a cup of tea, home-baked butter cookies, and share recipes. What I remember about Mary Jacoby were her homemade pies. Sister Anesia did not make many pies. But Mary knocked them out of the ballfield. The crust was so excellent, and her apple and peach pies were out of this world.

You are probably wondering at this point what has been going on with Chief of Detectives Teeling and his group working on the shootings. What I can tell you for certain is that in the depositions taken we know that Sarah Mitchell and her co-conspirators have a deep and abiding disgust for the Catholic Church. From what the lawyers have been able to determine when she was questioned under oath was that Bishop represents for them all that is wrong with the Church. Personally, they have a particular complaint about him as a priest and bishop. Yet for our area, he is the voice and the face of the Catholic

Church. In silencing him, they believe that they are striking a blow to the whole church. I know that our lawyers asked her if she did not realize they could kill Bishop Harrington, but within weeks after, Pope James would only appoint someone else to come in to shepherd the people of the diocese. Naturally, she knew that, but he would have paid for what he did, and if it took the killing of a few bishops, so be it. The one thing they were not able to get out of her was who else was involved and when their next attempt would be or where it would happen.

The partial fingerprint that was taken from the last envelope belonged to a James LaCross who was out of prison after serving years for attempted murder of a police officer. Whereabouts unknown to the FBI or local law enforcement. Even if Sarah Mitchell should be convicted, it still left LaCross out there and who knows how many more.

I told Bishop Harrington, as we were riding to work, that a couple of the nights I would cook dinner for the two of us. He looked skeptically at me, and asked, "When did you learn to cook, John?" I told him that Mom had insisted that all three of us know how to cook. Gert taught us how to get around in a kitchen and put a meal together. My brother and I had protested at the time, saying that was a women's job. But Mother reminded us that there was always the chance that we would need to cook if our wives were sick or died and so she was going to be sure that we were always okay, food-wise. Today I am happy that she spent the time to teach the three of us. Bishop suggested that I invite my mom over for dinner on one of those nights. I knew she would love it and told him I would do just that. Bishop had a great affection for his own mother, Margaret, and visited with her as often as he could before she died. He was also the first bishop of our diocese to have an annual Mass for the mothers of all the priests of the diocese followed by a luncheon. My mom has never missed a single one of the gatherings. Not only do they celebrate Mass with Bishop, have lunch with him, but he then takes the time to greet each one individually. Remarkably, as they come up and tell him who they are, he is able to say something to them about their son. How he remembers all that information is beyond me. The mothers love him for it. Just knowing that he was able to tell them about the work of their son, or his recent health scare, made them feel he was really concerned about their child.

Since the invitations were going out to clergy and public officials this week, I thought I had better call Jimmy Teeling and give him the dates. Today, I was lucky, because his secretary passed me right through to him. No hello from him, just a "No, we have nothing to report, if that is why you're call-ing, Father John." I was happy to let our chief of detectives know that was not the reason for my call, but rather to inform him of the dates of this year's celebration of our anniversary. I advised him that many bishops and cardinals from across the country would be attending both the concert and the Liturgy and dinner the next day. To say that Jimmy was not happy would be an understatement. He first asked if the chief knew about all this. I told him that his invitation was in today's mail.

Now I heard the voice of Detective James Teeling on the other end of the phone. You could actually hear the tone change, and he became very formal with me. I was informed that in light of the information previously given to me, how they thought the threat was against the Catholic Church all these high-ranking clergy were going to be a nightmare for the department. I was equally informed that he would be talking to the Chief of Police and the Superintendent that afternoon to voice his concerns. I interjected that I was sure no one would be foolish enough at such an event to try and kill Bishop Harrington. As best he could, without being disrespectful, Det. Teeling said to me, "You just don't get it, do you?"

"Get what?" I asked.

He then told me that if these individuals had as much hatred for the Church as they thought, all the bishops and cardinals would be in danger. He was no longer just concerned about our bishop but all of these men. At that moment, the blood drained from me, and I felt faint at my desk. No, I had not realized the danger everyone was going to be in if the time of the festivities they did not apprehend the persons. I simply thanked Det. Teeling for informing me of the risk everyone was going to be put in and that I would tell Bishop Harrington of his concern.

I immediately buzzed Rose and asked if she could slip me into seeing the Boss in between appointments. She told me she would see what she could do, but that his schedule looked tight right now.

After lunch, my phone rang, and it was Rose. Bishop's 2:25 PM meeting had just been canceled, and she could get me in then if I still wanted to see him before we went home. I told I would take it. So at 2:25 PM, I walked into his office. His face said he was not expecting me. "John, what can I do for you?" he asked. I told him about my morning conversation with Detective Teeling and of his concerns. Bishop became very serious and said to me that he did not want to put any other members of the hierarchy at risk and that we should reconsider the invites. I reminded him that they had already gone out. He just sat at his desk saying nothing for about two minutes. Looking back at me, Bishop finally said, "I think you had better get a letter off to all of them, informing them of the possible risk and tell them how much we would have liked having them here, but it might be better if they stayed home for this one." I was going to argue the point with Bishop but knew that there was no way he was knowingly going to risk the lives of any of his fellow bishops.

I went back to my office and began drafting the letter. It would take me two days to finish it to my satisfaction. I gave it to Rose so that Bishop could see it before it went out. He signed it and told Rose to have me send it out immediately. The next day, all the letters went out to every member of the hierarchy in the United States including the Apostolic Nuncio.

Two weeks after I had sent the letter out, we had over one hundred responses from individual bishops and cardinals. Every one of them personally wrote to Bishop Harrington and told him that they understood his concern, but it made them more committed to attending than ever before. He would not stand alone that weekend. They would stand with him as a sign of solidarity and that they were not going to be intimidated as Shepherds of the Roman Catholic Church in the United States of America. Even the Apostolic Nuncio called Bishop Harrington and personally told him that he would be present and had made the Holy Father aware of the situation. Pope James had promised his prayers for the safety of all and blessings on the diocese itself.

While we were having dinner this evening, I asked Bishop what we were going to do now that we knew more of his colleagues were coming than we originally could have imagined or planned for. Bishop told me that he had already called the rector of the seminary we have and it was agreed that the seminarians would be given that weekend off and they could hold up to two hundred bishops there. He had also decided that the Cardinals and Apostolic Nuncio, Archbishop Francesco Rossi, would stay at the Hilton, which is two blocks from the cathedral. He had Monsignor Thomas, the Vicar-General, book their rooms and put him in charge of making sure all their needs were met while here. Bob would be responsible for making sure cars were at the airport to pick them up when they arrived and get them back to the airport when the dinner was over. Msgr. Thomas also arranged that there would be a separate lounge for them to gather in at the Hilton.

It would be my job to keep the police department informed. Msgr. Bob Thomas has also arranged that all the bishops would be bussed back and forth from the Queen of Peace Seminary for the concert, meals, and Liturgy. The next day, I called Detective

Teeling and informed him of the resolve of the bishops and cardinals and where we were going to put them all up. He told me that he would tell the chief of police and that he was sure there would be ample police officers available to protect them. He recommended that a police escort leads the buses into the city and then back again after events. I told him I saw no issue with that and was most grateful for what the department was doing. I did tell him to let the chief know that Bishop would be sending a check for seven thousand dollars to help defray the cost of overtime. He was not sure that was sufficient but did not want the city to have to bear the full financial burden for an event of the Church. Detective Teeling was surprised and told me he was sure that the chief would appreciate the gesture.

We were now into the weeks that the Sisters were away on a needed rest and break from taking care of us all year long. The first night we had the lasagna meal brought by Mary Jacoby. The next night, I cooked, and as requested by Bishop, Mom was present. It was funny, here she was nervous. When Bishop was at the house, she was just honored to have him, but now she was sitting at his table, in the official residence of the bishop eating with him. It made me smile to see my mom being nervous. I had made a ham, scalloped potatoes, long green beans, beets, and croissants for the meal. Mom arrived about twenty minutes ahead of time and wanted to lend a hand. However, I put my foot down and told her the kitchen was only big enough for one cook at a time. I then led her into the front sitting room where Bishop was already present. Right away, he got up, went over, and gave Gert a kiss on the right cheek and asked what she would like to drink. She asked if he had rum and coke and indeed we did. I went back to the kitchen, and Bishop fixed her a drink as well as his own, which was bourbon on the rocks. I could hear laughter from the other room and wondered what they were talking about. Naturally, I would never find out. Dinner turned out great, and during the meal, my mom offered to come over one evening and cook for us. Before I could say anything, Bishop said that would be wonderful, but only if she agreed to eat again with us. Mom said she would be delighted, and it was decided that on Friday evening, she would do the cooking. She told us she would pick up whatever she needed so not to worry about getting stuff in for that night.

Before we knew it, the two weeks had come and gone, and Sister Kunegunda and Sister Anesia was back in the house. The first night they were home, Bishop asked them to join us after dinner and asked all about their time away. They told him that the trip was so special for them. Mother Veronica had made sure that not only were rooms available for them, but she also arranged for some of the sisters who trained at the same time they did were brought to the motherhouse. So at least for one of the weekends, they had a fabulous reunion all sharing what they were doing in their different ministries. Mother had arranged for two of the novices to drive them to various sights in South Carolina. Our sisters were not used to such attention and were overwhelmed by all of it. Mother took the time to meet with each of them personally, to hear how they were doing, what concerns they might have and assured them of the congregation's support. Both of our Sisters were so delighted that Bishop had made all this possible for them. I could tell, as they talked about their outings, their reunion that he was pleased it went so well. The next morning, after getting to the office, he called Mother Veronica and thanked her for making the time in South Carolina so unique for our two sisters. Mother told Bishop it was she who should be thanking him. She said how much each of the sisters thought of him. How utterly frightened they had been when the two attempts on his life had taken place. They also told their Superior General that Bishop had them share the Christmas meal with him, Fred, and myself. Mother Veronica said she could not begin to thank him enough for showing such respect and concern to two elderly religious women and she would keep him and the diocese in her prayers. Bishop assured her of his and that of the Congregation in his.

The next two months, Bishop would visit the parishes where he had not been able to Confirm our young adults last year. He is trying to complete everything before Lent begins. It is always tricky this time of year because of the weather. One never knows if a snowstorm will prevent travel or make it dangerous for families and friends to come out to celebrate the Liturgy and see their family member receive the Sacrament of Confirmation.

On the way home from the office today, Bishop told me that he had received a letter from the Apostolic Nuncio informing Bishop that our Holy Father was sending the Papal secretary of state, Ricardo Cardinal Navarro, from Rome to attend our celebration and that he would personally represent the pope. This hardly ever happened and Bishop was completely caught off guard. He called the nuncio right after reading the letter and invited him and Ricardo Cardinal Navarro, Secretary of State and former Archbishop of Mexico City to stay at the bishop's residence while visiting. The Nuncio said he would pass on the message and was sure the arrangement would be fine with Cardinal Navarro.

After dinner that night, I went right to my room and called our friend Detective Teeling to inform him of this change. He thanked me but said he would have to notify the United States State Department of the Papal Secretary of State coming to the city. He was sure that it would now be the state department who would meet him at the Washington Airport and would be providing a security detail for the time he was in the States. I had not thought of that, but as the second-ranking individual for the Vatican State, he was entitled to such protocol. Jimmy also said that the detail would probably be in charge, but that was something the Chief of Police would have to work out with the State Department for the two nights they would be staying here with us. It would mean Sister Kunegunda would have to have two of the guest rooms made up for the nuncio and the secretary. As long as she would not have to press his red cloak, she would be all right.

At times, it was like being on a merry-go-round. We were moving right along, up, and down on our carousel horses just enjoying the ride. Yet it was our carousel, we were in charge, and were responsible for everyone having an experience they would not forget. It did make my head spin at times just thinking of all we still had to do.

Chapter 8

I asked Bishop if it was all right with him if I took two weeks of my vacation time to go away and just get some needed rest and unwind. He asked when I was planning on going. I told Bishop Harrington that Father Lou, and I would be traveling together and he had the last two weeks of February set aside as vacation time. Bishop asked me to let Lou know he had no issue with my getting away, and he would ask Father Peter to act as his master of ceremonies for that period of time. Henry Peter had filled in for me on occasion in the past and was familiar with what Bishop expected and wanted during ceremonies. With his permission given for the time, I called Lou and told him I would be free. Louis asked me to let him handle everything, plane reservations, where we were going, and transportation back and forth to the airport. We have traveled a few times in the past, and I had no problems with Lou making all the arrangements. Just told him to make sure he told me if I would need clothing for a warm destination or a cold one. We could, with him choosing the destination, find ourselves on a tropical beach or the slopes of a ski resort. Three days later, Lou called and told me to pack my bathing suit. I did not ask where we were going, just thanked him for taking care of all the plans.

The day finally came, and an Uber car arrived in front of the residence with Father Lou in the back seat. I went out, the driver had already gotten out and opened the trunk so I could put my overhead bag in it. We were off for a holiday I know I needed. I did not realize it was one that Lou needed more than me.

We would be flying to the island of St. Lucia in the Caribbean for our stay. I, for one, had never been there before but had heard it had some of best reefs to go snorkeling in and fabulous beaches. What I did not know was how friendly the people of the island are. Wherever we went, you were greeted with warm smiles, hearty greetings, and warmth toward strangers you rarely find. Here you were treated like a relative they had not seen in a while. We did lots of swimming in the crystal-clear Caribbean Ocean. You can stand up in water to your neck and still see your feet it is so clean and clear. It made great snorkeling. Most nights we ate at one of the seven restaurants attached to the hotel we were staying in. The other nights we visited places recommended to us by the locals. I must say, eating at them was one of the highlights of the trip. The food was plentiful, the prices very cheap, and the music, singing was priceless.

I have known Lou since our seminary days, so I can see or sense when something is not right with him. One evening, we were just sitting on our balcony gazing out at the ocean and listening to the crashing of waves, I asked Lou what was eating at him. Had something happened at the parish or rectory that had him out of sorts? He assured me that there were no issues with the pastor and the other associate in the rectory. I nodded okay and keep looking at him, expecting him to say more. Lou just sat there, and I could see his eyes starting to tear up. I reached over and grabbed his hand in mine and assured him that I was there for him. He said he knew that, but it was still difficult sharing with me what was happening. We just sat there for about a half hour, neither of us saying a word when finally, he blurted out that he was having an affair with a woman from the parish. To say I was shocked, surprised are understatements. However, I knew that what I said or did next would either cement our close relationship or shatter it.

I asked Lou if she was married. He shook his head no. I then asked if she was of legal age or a minor? Thankfully, Lou said to me that she was a woman in her early thirties and never been married. "Do you believe, not feel, you love her?"

Again, he filled up and shrugged his shoulders. "I believe I love her," he said, "but I am not sure it is not infatuation. Sharon is beautiful, intelligent, funny, and a pleasure to be around he told me."

"How long have you been involved, Lou?"

"Just over a year," he responded.

"What are you going to do, if you know, at this point?"

Lou said one of the reasons he wanted the two of us to share this trip was for my advice in handling Bishop Harrington.

Here was my best friend and I knew what I was going to tell him would not be what he wanted to hear from me. I pushed our chairs next to one another and draped my arm over his neck and shoulders. "If you are going to seek laicization, I know that Bishop will do all he can for you in having Rome grant it. You know, Lou, ever since the bishops signed off on what is now known as the Texas Accord, no Bishop is allowed to keep a person in active ministry who is or has been in a sexual relationship with someone. I can tell you that he will put you on administrative leave, ask you to go for counseling. Bishop Harrington will also ask to meet with Sharon to hear her account of this relationship. If, in any way she feels that she was falsely led into it by you, or abused by you, I know he will offer her assistance as well to professionally sort it all out for her."

Lou assured me that it was not like that. He believed Sharon felt the same way about him as he did for her. So as we sat there on the balcony, I asked if he saw himself getting married to her. Lou just shook his head in the affirmative. When he finally spoke, he said it would have to be after his family and hers came to grip with it. Coming from a strong Hispanic community, Lou knew his mom was going to take the news hard. Plus, he would have to find a job that would be able to provide for them, or at least carry his own financial weight in the relationship. Lou has a Master's degree in counselling so that was an avenue he would be able to pursue. He would have to get his certification by the state, but I did not believe it would be a problem for him.

Lou then asked me if I would still be his friend after he left active ministry. I was caught off guard by it and all too quickly answered, "Naturally, I would be." As a married man, he would not be as free as he is now to go to dinner, the movies, vacations, or just to hear me out on a bad day. I knew he was right, that things would not be as they are right now, but I assured him we would remain friends. I also promised him that I would do all that I could to make the transition as easy as possible for him.

That night as we lay in our respective beds, I knew he was not sleeping as I lay there staring at the ceiling. Looking back, there had been signs, but I ignored them. Now it was incumbent on me to help him do what at one time in his and my life was unthinkable—namely, leave the priesthood. Actually, he will be leaving active ministry, even if he is laicized. The Catholic Church holds that once a man is ordained a priest, he is always a priest. All the Church can do is relieve him of his vow of celibacy and take away his faculties or license to practice ministry openly. However, if he ever came across a situation where someone was hurt or dying and were asking for a priest, and none were available, he could administer Sacraments to the individual. He could hear their confession, forgive the sins confessed, and he could administer the Sacrament of the Sick if he had the Oil of the Sick available to him. I would make sure that Lou always did. In all these cases, it is the Church that allows him to do it for the sake of the person in need. Most men who have been laicized never find themselves in such a situation.

As we were flying back, I said to Lou that I thought he should make an appointment with

Bishop, after talking to Sharon, and let him know what his intentions were. Lou stated that he would and asked that I be present when he told Bishop Harrington. I told my best friend that would be highly unusual, but if it meant it was the only way he could get through, it I surely would be there with him. Lou thanked me, not just for that, but for always having his back over the past twenty-five plus years. I assured him that, to the extent that I could, I always would be there for him.

True to his word, on Monday he called Rose and made an appointment to see Bishop on Wednesday morning at eleven. He then called me to let me know. I had an internal office meeting to attend but called and excused myself from it.

When I returned to the bishop's residence, Bishop was there to greet me. Delighted to have me back and noting the nice tan I had and how rested I seemed. I told him that Lou and I had a great time and how beautiful the island and people of St. Lucia where. Bishop listened intently and then said it was good to have me back. He also said much of the final plans had been completed for the anniversary celebration and that I should call Detective Teeling and get an update from him on the investigation. I asked him how Father Henry Peters had made out as his master of ceremonies and Bishop smiled and told me he had done fine. However, he was no John

Writerson. One of his best compliments on the job
I did for him.

On Monday morning, after greeting the staff
on my return, I did call Detective Jimmy Teeling and
was told he would be out most of the day. He was
testifying in a murder case, and his secretary expected
him not to be back into the office. I thanked her and
asked that she just leave a note that I called and if he
could get back to me at his convenience that would
be great.

The day arrived when Lou was coming into
see Bishop. He arrived at my office at ten fifty and
told me he was really nervous about telling the Boss
about his situation. I assured him that I knew from
previous experience with our priests that Bishop
was very sensitive to both the needs of the priest
involved as well as the other person(s). I asked Lou
to hear Bishop out and not to overreact to anything
he said.

At eleven o'clock, Lou knocked on the outer
door to Bishop's office, and he could hear him say,
"Come in." Lou and I walked in together. Seeing
both of us before him, Bishop Harrington knew
this was not a social visit, nor was it about something minor. He invited both of us to sit down. We
did, and Bishop took his seat in the corner of the
room to the left of his desk. He always sat there

with this overhead light shining down on him. It was a strange sight and arrangement, but Bishop found that he could see better this way. His vision was not the best, and even with glasses, he did have some difficulty if the light was just not right. He asked Lou what was up and my friend proceeded to tell him everything that he had shared with me. A couple of times he choked up, and I rested my hand on his shoulder. Finally, he finished and just sat there looking at the man who held his fate in his hands. Bishop asked him some questions about Sharon and their relationship up to this point. When Lou responded, he was candid and calm.

In years gone by, the individual Bishop had more leeway in how situations like this were to be handled. However, since the sex scandals with priests engaging in illegal activities with minors the National Conference of Bishops has taken a firm position and implemented policies that all dioceses throughout the country are to comply with and implement. It has become known as the Texas Accord since it was finalized at their annual meeting that was held in Texas that year. Now, any clergy who have been involved in sexual activity with a woman, man, or minor has to be removed from active ministry. Bishop explained, in a gentle voice, that he was going to put Lou on administrative leave with pay, but he wanted Lou to go to a treatment center in Maryland to process all that had taken place and would be occurring in the future. Since Lou had already asked Bishop to begin the laicization process so that he would be able to enter into the Sacrament of Matrimony with Sharon, Bishop assured him that he would start the paperwork that had to be sent to Rome. The Boss told Lou that within the next two days, he would receive an official letter from him about all of this. He also suggested that Lou move to his family home until it was time for him to leave for the treatment center. Lou Santiago agreed and gave Bishop the address of his mom's house. Bishop also asked Lou to have Sharon call to meet with him if she was agreeable to such a meeting. He assured Bishop that he had already brought it up to her and she had no issue with seeing Bishop face-to-face.

Bishop got up and walked over to Lou who had stood as he saw Bishop coming toward him. Bishop embraced him, thanked him for the years of service that he had given to the diocese, for being such a good friend to me, and assured him that he would always be available if Lou ever wanted to talk, even after he was laicized and married. Bishop also told him that if he and Sharon wanted he would like to be at their wedding. Lou teared up at that and only shook his head in agreement, and we left the office. We stopped in my office where my best friend broke down and cried. I just held him in my arms until the sobbing ended. When we looked into each other's eyes, I knew his pain and felt it with him. We both understood that we would always be there for each other, just different now. Finally, he broke free and said he had to get his stuff together and move it to his mother's house. I asked if he wanted me to come and give him a hand, but he said he thought it would be best if he did it alone. He wanted to tell the pastor and the other associate about his decision and what was going to happen. It was one of the saddest days of my life. I loved Lou as a brother and hated seeing him hurting. Yet I knew that if he was right about Sharon, and I had every reason to feel he was, she would be there throughout the next few months giving him the support he would need.

That evening, as Fred drove us home, Bishop looked over at me and said, "That was the right thing for you to do today, being there to support your best friend. I know you are hurting tonight, John, but know there was no other choice available and I am here for you as well." I thanked him for his kindness, gentleness with Lou, and especially for thanking him for all the good he had done in over twenty-five years of active ministry. We made the rest of the trip home in silence. Each of us lost in our own thoughts and prayers.

Five days later, Lou was on the road to Maryland and the start of the therapeutic program the diocese had arranged. I prayed that it would be good for him and that he would be able to address not only the issue that brought him there but any other that could hinder or limit his being the best husband and father that he could possibly be. I knew that he would do his part, but that it would still be a painful process for him. Sharon accompanied him to Maryland and then drove Lou's car back here. She reminded him that she would be waiting to drive him back whenever he called for her to get him.

Chapter 9

The diocese continued firming up the arrangements for our anniversary celebration. I had the chance, the other evening, to hear the combined adult and youth choirs practice at the cathedral. Here we have the 150 voices of our young people and the eighty-voice adult choir. In the three-joint hymns they are going to do, it was amazing how their voices filled the entire cathedral. I cannot even begin to adequately describe to you how marvelous the sound is. The choir master of the cathedral has written a special anniversary hymn that will be sung during the offertory procession. It is an accurate reflection of our history and the deep-abiding faith of the people. It is titled "Raise your hands in Prayer, O Faithful People of God." Bishop has not heard it, and I am sure he will be so proud and elated by this rendering of our anniversary hymn. The rector, Msgr. Bob, and I had just gone over all the planning for the Mass. The two days will be a real strain on his staff. They have to have the sanctuary set up for the concert the night before, and as soon as it is over, everything has to be taken down, and the sanctuary has to be ready for the masses the next morning and the Jubilee or Anniversary Mass later that day. On top of all those arrangements, Bob was working closely with the local TV station that would be broadcasting the entire Liturgy. He also had to make sure that the police departments requests were being properly handled. Msgr. Bob did not approve of guns in the cathedral but realized the necessity of the police having sharpshooters and others present in light of the attempts on the life of our bishop. He had shown them, unknown to the public, walkways that were behind the ceiling of the cathedral. Many of the air vents would give the sharpshooters perfect shots of someone in the pews that day, or as we experienced last time, walking up to receive Communion. I told him that ever since the Knights of Columbus Liturgy we could not take for granted any gathering would be a safe place. In light of so many members of the hierarchy being present, it was even more imperative that we err on the side of caution. The state department would also have personnel here to guard the Papal secretary of state. Then there would be the state police present since the governor has already responded that he and his wife would attend the Mass and the dinner.

I went this past Wednesday to visit Lou. It was emotional for both of us. Lou told me that he was okay and doing his best in being honest with the therapists. He was dealing with some family of origin issues that came up during the sessions. Lou told me that he appreciated our friendship more now than ever before. He realized that in life we have many individuals who come into our lives, claiming to be our friend, yet when the chips are down, they are not seen or heard from. I told him I thought that maybe they just did not know what to say or how to act. Lou just looked at me and said, "You knew what to say, not say, and when to hold me." I just nodded my head that it was a no-brainer for me. Lou told me that he had called Sharon and told her what he was learning about himself and asked her to try and get to know me better. He wanted her to realize that I was not a threat to their relationship. That he loved me, like no other male, and he would continue seeing and loving me. She told him that she understood and had two girlfriends that she was as close with as he seemed to be with me. If he were not jealous of them or the time she spent with them, she would have no issue with him seeing me when he needed to do that.

I just hugged my best friend and told him that I felt the same for him. Bishop Harrington, I informed Lou, sent his best to him, and wanted Lou to know he was keeping him in prayer. Lou asked me to thank him for his concern. Also told me to thank him for the two hours he had spent with Sharon.

Apparently, when she came to see Bishop, they both talked, questioned one another, and before they knew it, the two hours had slipped by. Rose had, as she always did, guarded her Boss, and made sure appointments were changed, canceled as the time ticked away. When the two of them emerged from Bishop's office, it was said you could hear the sigh of relief from Rose clear down the hallway. Lou related how Sharon found Bishop so easy to talk with, not intimidating at all. He offered her whatever support he could and told her how he would like to be at the wedding if at all possible. She promised him that he would receive an invitation. It has just been assumed by everyone that I would be the official witness of the marriage for the church and the celebrant of the Liturgy.

As I was driving back home, I remembered all the times—good and bad—that Lou and I shared together. He always had my back, and I tried to do the same for him. We studied together for exams while in the seminary. Each quizzing the other on what we thought would be contained on the examination. How our families were present when we received Minor Orders, and then for the days we were ordained Sub-deacons and Deacons. Since we were ordained to the Priesthood on the same day and had our first Mass the next day, we could not concelebrate with one another. Probably the only major event we did not share together. Now his journey would take him on an entirely new road, one I never traveled. My heart said nothing between us would be different. However, my brain told me things would be different once he was married and if he and Sharon had children.

Bishop was already asleep by the time I arrived back at the residence. I would share with him at breakfast what Lou wanted me to convey and generally how Lou was making out.

Lieutenant Detective James Teeling called me on Thursday morning just as I was entering my office. He wanted to update me on the investigation. Federal and local officers assigned to the case were now convinced that there were possibly three individuals involved. On top of that, they were equally sure that the next, maybe the final attempt, would be the weekend of the jubilee celebration of our 150th anniversary of the founding of this diocese. As a result, Jimmy wanted us to know, that security was going to be raised to its highest-level days before the two days of scheduled activities. The airport security and police were brought in so that the bishops who were flying in and out would be protected. A lounge had been set aside for them. As we had enough to fill one of the buses taking them to the seminary, they would move from the room to the bus. The Cardinals were being taken immediately to the Hilton. Msgr. Bob Thomas had that all in place with their scheduled times of arrival. The Papal Nuncio and the Papal secretary of state would be coming in from Washington, DC, by limo. They would be brought right to the bishop's residence where police will already be on duty outside.

I thanked Jimmy for keeping me informed and that I would pass the information onto Bishop, the Vicar-General, and jubilee committee. He also told me that they had one person under observation as a person of interest in the planned attacks on Bishop Harrington. If that was the case, there was really only one unknown person since Sarah Mitchell who fired the first bullet at Bishop was constantly under observation.

Bishop was scheduled for his annual vacation in March. He always got together with two of his seminary classmates and another bishop friend each year. One of them made the arrangements for all. This year, like most, the days would be filled with rounds of golf. In the evening, they usually played cards, watched movies, or listened to Joe play the piano. Joe could not read music but had a musical ear. If you could hum a song or sing it, he could play it. And so, the four of them would gather together, drinks in hand, and have a sing-along. I always found it difficult seeing Bishop participating in a sing along or playing cards. It just was not the image he projected when out and about in the diocese. For those two weeks, he was just Wally, one of the boys and he liked it like that. As I had needed my time away, I knew that Bishop Harrington needed this time away from the diocese more than in any other year.

Happy to report that Bishop is back with us again. He is looking tanned and rested. Last evening Bishop told me that over the two weeks, he won twice while golfing and had some high Pinochle Hands. The best part was that he was able to reconnect with old friends and that meant a great deal to him.

Our city, like many large cities, has its fair share of drive-by shootings, gang shootings or robberies went wrong, and someone dies. Last evening, around nine o'clock, three children were killed in a drive-by shooting. They were just outside playing in their front yards when the bullets started flying. Who the intended target was, the police have no idea right now. It could have been one of the parents sitting on the porch watching the kids, one of the teenagers who were out and about, all that still had to be determined.

Two of the three children attend one of our parish schools. The pastor had called me early this morning to inform me and that the superintendent was sending in counselors for the children and staff members who would need their services. The pastor, Father Bill Wiggins, has only been there for two years. He teaches religion to the seventh- and eighth-grade students and has been actively involved in the life of the school. This shooting hit him hard since one of the children was one of his seventh-grade students, the other from the fifth-grade class. I told Bill that I would let Bishop know and keep us informed about funeral arrangements.

Bishop, during the masses at the high schools, talked about gun violence and the need to be peace-makers and not indiscriminate killers. Having been shot at twice, and hit once, I knew this would affect him deeply. Bishop at least had a bulletproof vest on to protect him, these three children had nothing to protect them from random violence.

When I told Bishop Harrington about Father Bill Wiggins call he said he would call him this morning and make sure he was coping. I suggested he have Rose call the school if he wanted to talk with him since I was sure that is where he would be spending most of the day.

Rose called the rectory first, at Bishop's direction, only to be told by the secretary that Father Bill was over at the school. The secretary at the school did page him, and he and Bishop spoke for about ten minutes. Father Bill asked if Bishop would be attending the funeral and he was assured that Bishop would be there. However, he would not be the principal celebrant of the Mass since he felt Bill should be the one. The children all knew and were at ease with Father Bill and Bishop did not want the funeral Liturgy to be any harder than it normally would be. Bishop told him that he would do the final blessing and prayers over the coffin at the end of the Mass. Father Bill thanked him for both his willingness to be present and to participate.

The parents informed Father Bill that the wake would be on Friday afternoon and evening with the funeral Liturgy on Saturday morning at ten o'clock. All three were going to be laid out in the largest funeral home we have here in the city. Then the two bodies of our students will be brought to the parish church for the Liturgy. The third child was Lutheran, and the Liturgy for him would take place at King of Peace Lutheran Church.

On Thursday, Chief of Detectives Teeling was on the phone with me and told me that they had arrested the man they believed was one of the co-conspirators in the attempted killing of Bishop. He reminded me that for the last couple of weeks, they had him under surveillance. Last evening he was arrested for the attempted armed robbery of a liquor store. Jimmy Teeling said it would be enough to keep him off the street at the time of the Jubilee which was fast approaching. They did not believe he would be able to post bail so he would be sitting in the county jail until his trial date.

It was now down to Sarah our first shooter, who knew she was closely watched and our unknown individual. The FBI profiler had given us a picture of what he believed was a very smart person, probably male, in his late thirties or early forties, who had some major event take place in his life of which he felt the Catholic Church was responsible. Honestly, I told Jimmy, I could not see how that helped us at all. We had a male in this thirties or forties, probably white who had a real grudge against the Church. Our dear detective friend could have been describing a third of all who would attend the jubilee concert, Mass, or dinner. Jimmy admitted it was like looking for a needle in a haystack. However, if the light hit that needle right, it would stand out, and that was what they were hoping. All agencies hoping that one of their agents or sharpshooters would catch a glimmer of that needle and either take it out or have agents move in and arrest the individual.

I knew that Bishop Harrington would want the person arrested if at all possible. He would not want anyone killed at one of the three major events of the jubilee. Only time would tell if that would be possible.

We did attend the funeral Liturgy that Saturday. Father Bill gave an excellent homily/sermon during the Mass. I believe most of the inner city priests concelebrated the Liturgy. Bishop did the final commendations over the two coffins. He then met privately in the sacristy of the church with both families and shared their grief and sorrow over this senseless act of violence. He did not spend much time with them since they had to go to the cemetery for the burial. However, it was enough for the families that Bishop was present and held each one of them in his embrace. There was not a dry eye in the room.

Fred McNamara drove us back to the residence. Bishop did not have anything else scheduled for this evening or tomorrow, so we were both free to catch up on other work.

I called my buddy Lou who was now home from the treatment center. He was living with his mom. As soon as he picked up the phone, he announced that Mom wanted me to come for dinner and that she would not take "no" for an answer. And so it was agreed that I should come about five and we would eat at six. Lou and I would be able to spend quality time with each other, and that is what was needed. We knew that his mom would leave us two alone so going to his house was the best place to meet.

During the evening, Lou told me that he had learned a great deal about himself while he was there. Sharon had already commented on how he seemed to be more in touch with his inner feelings now. Women always seem to be more aware of feelings than men are. Sharon was pleased with how easily he talked, not just about stuff, but how he felt about it all. As a result, she was able to share more deeply with him.

I learned that evening that they were planning a wedding for the end of the summer if all the paperwork had come through from Rome and his laicization was in hand. I assured Lou that Bishop had sent in all the needed work from his office and asked that he be expedited.

Lou wanted to know if there had been any new threats made against Bishop or attempts on his life while he was away. I told him we had been lucky so far and everything was quiet. Almost too quiet I realized after I had said it. Almost like the eye of a hurricane, where there is a calm, a stillness before the worst of the storm strikes. I prayed God that was not going to be the case for the diocese or Bishop Harrington.

I did not leave until about eleven that night. There is a closeness between us that can accommodate either of us being away, and when we are together again, it is as if we just saw each other the day before. That is how it was last evening with Lou and me.

On Monday morning, following up on my conversation with Lou, I called Detective Teeling to tell him how it dawned on me that it had been too quiet of late. Jimmy laughed when he heard me say it to him. He asked if was envious of his job and wanted to be a detective now. I assured him that I did not but could not wonder why Sarah or our unknown person had not tried to contact Bishop again. Jimmy Teeling informed me that they had always wondered about that also. It was not a good sign that there had been no new notes, communications in any form since the last one.

Just as I hung up, the intercom buzzer went off. It was Rose telling me that Bishop wanted to see me in his office immediately. I instantly went down the hall, knocked, and entered at his beckoning. He was holding an envelope up with his letter opener. Apparently, he had not opened it. Right away I knew it was from our would be killer(s). When I went to his desk, Bishop asked me to look at the handwriting. It was similar to the writing on the previous envelopes. Bishop put it down, buzzed Rose, and asked her to go to the cafeteria and get a plastic bag and two pairs of the gloves they wore when serving food. Without questioning him, Rose went and returned with the bag and two sets of gloves. Bishop put one set on and handed me the other. He then proceeded to slit open the envelope and remove the paper inside. He looked at it and handed it over to me.

The message was short and to the point.

"Your hour has come. You will soon meet your Lord and God. This is the last time you will hear from us."

There it was! Whatever was going to happen was going to occur shortly. From Bishop's office, I called Detective Teeling who said he would be right over.

Our security guard Henry escorted Detective Teeling up to the office. First thing, after he kissed Bishop's ring was to ask if we had touched either the envelope or letter. Bishop showed him the plastic gloves we wore, and Jimmy was pleased that we had used them. He read the note, bagged it, and said it was a good sign. At least there was movement again, and he would inform all local and federal authorities of the latest communication.

Since we were now only three weeks before the jubilee celebration, my gut said whatever was going to go down, would probably occur during those days. It would be the worst of times in the way of protection. So many visitors, individuals attending the different functions it would be hard to pinpoint who the shooter or shooters would be. We knew that there were at least three people involved, but what if there were more? This communique told us it was the last time that we would hear from "us." Was that "us" the three of them, or was that "us" more than we recently knew?

Chapter 10

Everything seemed to be moving at a feverish pace in these last weeks before the jubilee celebrations. I knew that the choir had finally chosen what it was going to be wearing. All would be in blue choir robes, with a gold panel coming down each side of the front. The young people's choir had a white panel down the front. The combined numbers they would do should have the congregation breathless after hearing them. They really were that good. I could not get over the change since the first time I heard them.

All the vestments had arrived that the concelebrations would be wearing. We had requested that the Bishops and Cardinals attending wear white miters for the Liturgy. For the jubilee concert, they would all be in what is termed their choir cassock. Bishop Harrington would be the only one wearing the choir cassock with the addition of a surplice and a short cape that goes over the shoulders, the mozzetta. The five Cardinals that would be attending will wear, well whatever they want as Cardinals of the Church. I knew that at least three of them would be wearing, over their choir cassock, the crimson five-meter-long cape or cappa magna. They all will wear their scarlet watered-silk red birettas over the scarlet skull cap/zucchetto.

Next week all the involved law enforcement agencies that are working together will be here to see where they want to place people and sharpshooters. The local television station has been here twice now determining the best placement of cameras, sound equipment, and extra lighting if needed for clear video. This past Wednesday, Jimmy Teeling had two of his team over to the residence to see the rooms the Papal Nuncio and the Vatican Secretary of State would be staying in while here with us. This way, from outside the building, those rooms would be especially under watch. We were informed that during their actual stay, Secret Services officers would be inside the house providing additional protection. We were told that they would not need rooms or meals. Because they worked on shifts, their whole concentration would be the protection of those they were charged to watch.

Jimmy's two detectives also walked the garden area in the back of the residence. At this time of year, the flowers are just starting to bloom after a long winter's rest. It is a lovely place to relax in, just sit back and read, or as Bishop Harrington always says, a place for him to clear his head. Hopefully, our two guests will be able to utilize the garden during down periods of non-scheduled events.

I, for my part, really have little to do or prepare for in reality. I have no role in the concert the night before. I will be the official master of ceremonies for the Eucharistic Liturgy, and then just a paying guest at the jubilee or anniversary dinner.

Bishop does have one major event next Saturday. The Knights of Columbus are celebrating this year their 150th anniversary of their organizations founding. A Mass had been scheduled months in advance to celebrate this milestone with such a loyal group of men who have dedicated their lives, good works, to benefiting the Catholic Church. The Mass is going to be celebrated here in the cathedral the Saturday before the big jubilee Liturgy of the diocese's anniversary. The adult choir for the Jubilee has agreed to be present and sing. It will give them, if you will, a live dress rehearsal, for the next weekend. It will also give the law enforcement agencies a chance to have their people in place when the cathedral is filled to see how clear the sight lines are when it is crowded and people are moving about.

I believe that I forgot to tell you Lou and Sharon have set the date of their wedding. It will take place in Sharon's parish church on September 23 at 2:00 PM. Bishop and I both received our invitations just the other day. I already knew since I have been doing the paperwork for it. Lou had received his papers of laicization three weeks ago, signed them, and that cleared the last hurdle for the two of them entering into a valid Sacramental Marriage.

Everything the diocese could do in preparation for the two days of celebrations has been done. Everything is set at the Hilton; the seminary has all the arrangements in place to have the rooms made up as soon as the seminarians depart. The buses are all hired, police escorts are assigned, and the routes clear to everyone. The mayor also has three ambulance companies on duty the two days, just in case their services are needed for whatever reason.

Sister Kunegunda, OC, has already made up the rooms and baths for the Nuncio and Secretary of State to stay in while they are here. Sister Anesia, OC, has the Saturday evening planned so that we will be finished in sufficient time to go over to the concert. Fred is going to drive the Secretary of State and Papal Nuncio, and I will drive Bishop Harrington over. Since the chief of police has insisted that we have a full police escort, the trip over will hardly take us any time. In some ways, I feel like a kid in a candy shop who is just giddy with delight. I never have had the roads cleared for me in my life, so this is going to be a first.

Bishop Harrington has been working for weeks on the homily he will give when the Knights of Columbus gather, and then he has the homily at the jubilee, plus greeting remarks before the Liturgy begins. He will also speak at the formal dinner. I am sure when it is all over, Bishop Harrington will have lost at least five pounds just from perspiration. The pressure will be on him to set the tone for these particular gatherings, but also to make sure he is faithful to the Gospel message in calling us to live it out in our daily lives. Not any easy task under normal circumstances, but these are not normal times. Because of the attempts on his life, 198 of his fellow bishops from across the country are attending in solidarity with him. Plus, we have the five Cardinals and Nuncio participating. That means that virtually the majority of the hierarchy of the Church in the United States will be listening to every word he shares and making their own judgments about this man who is our bishop. I know, from the few things he has said at meals, that he is acutely aware of the pressure on him. The Nuncio and the Papal Secretary of State will both be reporting back to Pope James about what they experienced and what they heard. On top of all that, I knew that every minute they all were with us, Bishop Harrington would be worried about their safety. He had resigned himself that his own days were probably numbered. Lucky so far, but for how long that would continue was debatable. The thought that some other bishop or cardinal had been hurt or killed because they stood by him in this turbulent time was more than he wanted to carry. There was nothing I could do to put him at ease. My chest had not been black and blue and sore to touch for weeks after the bullet hit the vest he was wearing. He would always know that feeling, the force of the bullet trying to penetrate his bullet-proof vest.

Usually, when the Fourth-Degree Knights are present, they lead the procession and then stand along the edges of the church pews for the clergy and Bishop to pass by with their drawn swords. Since they still felt responsible for not having protected Bishop more at their previous celebration, they pleaded with us to allow them to walk on either side of Bishop in the procession. Oh yes, there would be the ones assigned for the church pews, but another set of Knights, mostly state officers would form the special honor guard around Bishop Harrington. In the mind of the Knights, there would be no repeat of the previous gathering. Bishop finally gave permission, for this one time, to allow them to form such an honor guard.

As the trumpets blared and the chorus raised its voices, the procession began to enter into the cathedral proper. True to their word, the Knights provided a very tight closed honor guard around Bishop. In fact, with their plumed hats, it was hard to even see Bishop coming down the aisle. All you could see was his miter in between all the feathers and drawn swords. At one point, I caught the eye of Bishop, and he just rolled his eyes at me. I knew he was totally embarrassed by this display of protective force being provided to him. At the same time, utterly grateful to these men who were willing to risk their lives for him.

The cathedral was packed. We had people standing in the aisles. If there was such a thing as a dress rehearsal for us and law enforcement, this was a good example of what it would be like next weekend at the concert and the Liturgy.

Bishop's homily was just about twelve minutes long and exceptionally uplifting, challenging, and filled with gratitude for all the Knights have done for the Church since their founding one hundred and fifty years ago.

The distribution of Holy Communion was a tense time for us. This was when Sarah had taken her shot at the chest of Bishop. The acolytes were again police officers who watched every moment, especially eye movement of those coming up for Communion. This time we were able to distribute the consecrated bread and wine without incident to the relief of many including all the Knights of Columbus. After the Mass, as is his custom, Bishop stood at the top of the Cathedral steps and greeted everyone who came out those big bronze doors. They were all delighted to shake his hand or kiss his ring, and he was in his element in the midst of his flock. All in all, it was a beautiful day and celebration.

Later that night, Detective Teeling called me to say they felt pretty good about next weekend. The sharpshooters said, despite the movement of people or those in the aisles, they felt they still had an excellent view and clear shots if they were called for. I prayed that they would never have to shot someone inside the cathedral.

The first couple of days in this the week of the celebrations were filled with radio and TV interviews that Bishop and the Vicar-General gave.

The jubilee committee believed everything was in place. Greeters were assigned to meet the bishops as they arrived at the airport and take them to the lounge until there were enough of them to fill one of the buses. Msgr. Thomas and Fred McNamara would be getting the Cardinals who were flying in. Three out of the five were driving and would go right to the Hilton and check in to their assigned suite. Bishop and I were feeling that finally, we were in a position where we could enjoy the next couple of days.

On Thursday afternoon, there was a loud explosion noise, the chancery building actually shook, things fell off of shelves, and there was a lot of screaming. I was not sure if it was our building, or what was happening.

When I got up from my desk chair and looked out the window, I could see billowing black smoke about two blocks or so from the chancery. Instantly, my mind began to try and picture what was in that area. I know there was one factory, a car dealership, homes, one of our elementary schools, stores, and a place that made cleaning supplies. The cleaning supply place had been cited previously for some safety violations, and I wondered if that was where the explosion had taken place. You could now hear the blare of fire engines, police car, and ambulance sirens rushing to the site of the blast.

When I went out of the office to see if everyone was okay, I saw Bishop Harrington rushing down the hallway. He was pure white and in a real hurry. I started to keep pace with him as I asked what was wrong. Bishop told me he had just gotten the call that the explosion had taken place at our elementary school, and there were many casualties. He was joining the local priests going over to anoint those who were injured and comfort the children, teachers, and parents as they waited to see who was alive and who had died or been wounded in the explosion.

Fred had the door open for Bishop as soon as we emerged from the building, and as soon as we were belted in the back seat, Fred took off toward the school.

The Fire-Police had cones lined up across the street about a block and a half away from the school. No one was being let through except first responders. Bishop stuck his head out the window and in the firmest of voices said to the fire-policeman that he was the bishop of this diocese, it was one of our schools, and if he did not let us through immediately, he would hear from the Chief of Police and the Mayor. The man looked at Bishop and moved the cones that were blocking the road and allowed us to go through.

To say what we saw was pure chaos would be an understatement. I am not sure what a war zone looks like, but this had to be close. Windows were blown out in buildings as far away as a block from the school. You could see where the force of the explosion had damaged buildings and homes near the school. About one-third of the school building was gone. There was just an area of massive debris where that part of the school had been. Fires were raging in the next section of the school; as well as nearby stores and homes. Because of monthly fire drills, the teachers who were not in the part that was missing had gotten their students out. But almost all of them were hysterically crying and trying to understand what had happened to their school and friends.

I saw at least ten of our priests hurrying through the bodies that were all over. Some without limbs, others already dead. They were anointing those still alive, moving from one to the other, to reach as many as they could. Bishop was already down on one knee anointing a teacher who was missing a right leg. I could see the tears running down his face as he prayed over and placed the Oil of the Sick on her forehead. I pulled out of my own stock and began to join my fellow priests in the anointing. We knew that was our first task, then we would start comforting the parents, children who lost a loved one today.

I cannot tell you how long we were there. It seemed like it was forever. I have never anointed so many in my life. Nor have I cried as much as I did today. It will be a long time before this community is able to recover. For some, there will be no recovery, just funeral masses, and burials. Many others will have months and years of physical therapy, psychological counseling before they can move on. The children and teachers who were burned will go through many skin grafts and never feel the same again. Today, innocence was lost, faith challenged, and a community left in complete shock and bewilderment.

It would take two days before the fire department had the last of the embers out. Fire Marshals were on scene sifting through the rubble to determine the exact cause of the explosion. More than likely, a natural gas leak, but that was not confirmed as of yet. Whatever, it would make little difference to those who sustained injuries or had endless nightmares as a result. Our insurance company was one of the first on site to assess the damages and determine who was at fault. Was it the gas company, the school, human error, or some mechanical failure that was the necessary spark to bring this destruction about.

When we finally arrived home, Bishop went right up to his room. He had said nothing on the ride home. From time to time, I saw out of the corner of my eye, a new tear run down his face. He looked like he had aged a good ten years. My head still could clearly hear the screaming, crying, wailing of sirens—sounds that would haunt me for weeks.

The next morning at breakfast, Bishop informed me that last night he had canceled the jubilee concert, Mass, and formal dinner. Bishop Harrington said he could not hold days of celebrations when so many in the city would be in mourning or sitting at bedsides with their loved ones in hospitals and burn units throughout the city. Bishop had called Cardinal Wolfgang and explained his decision. The Cardinal said he would tell the Nuncio who should be able to just about stop the Papal Secretary of State before he boarded his plane in Rome to Washington, DC, Cardinal Wolfgang would call the other Cardinals and all their staffs would alert the rest of the countries bishops of the cancellation and reason why. He told his friend Wally that whenever the celebrations would be rescheduled for that, he would clear his calendar and make sure he was present. Cardinal Wolfgang felt all those who said they were coming would do the same. He agreed now was not the time for celebrations, but a time for mourning and rebuilding. A time for healing and forgiving. It would have to be a time of comforting and a vision of the future.

I think I was so stunned that Bishop had done all this last evening that I just sat there at the table saying nothing. He asked me if I was okay, and I told him that I probably was not. Then like the father of all his priests, he said that I should arrange to have all those who were at the school anointing, comforting families come here to the residence and share with one another what they were going through.

Bishop said he would make sure that grief therapists would be present to assist in processing what each man was feeling.

As we were getting up from the table, Bishop Harrington told me that I was not going into work today or the next couple of days until the gathering of all the clergy who participated had taken place and that was an order. He has never ordered me to do anything over these five plus years. Bishop has asked me or told me to do many things and tasks but never once has he ordered me. Since I promised both obedience and respect to my ordaining bishop and all his successors, I just shook my head in agreement. I then went up to my room, which Sister Kunegunda has just finished cleaning and making the bed. I plopped down in my chair and cried. I could feel my shoulders shaking, I was crying so hard. All the built-up emotions just poured out of me. I wanted it over and done with. I wanted the pain to stop, the horrid pictures to go away. Yet I knew there were individuals out there who had no hands to wipe the tears away because of the explosion. I understood that this was a shared pain and that I had better start making those phone calls to the other priests. Bishop knew that we all would not be of any help to the people we serve if we did not deal with this tragedy ourselves. By lunchtime, I had contacted everyone, and it was agreed that on Tuesday, we would meet here at the residence.

When Bishop came home that evening, I went down to his room, before dinner, and told him that I had contacted everyone, and next Tuesday, we would gather here at the house. He asked me straight out how I was holding up. I told him how I had totally lost it this morning after he left. Never had I felt so helpless or alone. The bishop understood and reminded me that I was not alone and he had no intention of allowing me to be overtaken by what we all had experienced. He told me that when he had served as a chaplain during the Vietnam war; he had seen way too much death and violence for a lifetime. Those battles to this day could still bring him, at times of stress, nightmares. Yesterday had reminded him of those days, of the wounded, dead soldiers he had to be present to and assist. Bishop wanted me to know that it was all right to have the feeling that I did, but necessary to share them and not keep them bottled up inside of me.

I thanked him for what he said, but just for being himself with me. He was a very compassionate, kind, forgiving man and one I was proud to work for each day.

Since we could not cancel the caterers in time, the food that was prepared for the formal dinner was distributed to all the soup kitchens and shelters throughout the city. It went, not just to the ones we run, but to every one of them no matter who ran

or sponsored them. Those who had purchased tickets were told they would receive their money back,
but in light of all that happened, it was best that we
reschedule at some later date and that the food was
going to the shelters and food kitchens. Over half
of the dinner guests told us to keep the money.

On Tuesday, we did come together and spend
three hours just sharing, being led through a process
of healing by the grief therapists. There was a good
deal of crying, anger being expressed, but also a
renewed sense of purpose and solidarity among us.
We were called to serve and not in just the best of
times. It would always be our mission to bring healing to the wounded that no medical doctor could do.
As priests, we had to bring not ourselves to events
like we just went through, but Jesus who offers not
only healing but life to all who believe. Jesus never
promised we would not suffer, actually He makes
clear that we will if we follow Him. What He does
promise is that those who keep His teachings and
are open to the Will of His Father will be with Him
in the Kingdom of God. That is our mission in this
city, this diocese, and this church that we minister in.
We are to be that beacon of light that leads all to a
safe place.

Chapter 11

Wednesday, the day after our gathering, the funerals began. By the end of next week, there would be over fifty funeral masses celebrated, not counting another twenty for students who were not Roman Catholic but attended our school. Bishop Harrington attended all he could of the Funeral Liturgies, as well as those held by other faiths as his schedule permitted. For our city, our churches, the community it was a heart-wrenching time. Never before in the history of this great city had we experienced such a tragedy. Fifty-seven children and three teachers perished in that explosion. Some thirty more lost limbs or were burnt. All classes had been suspended in our Catholic schools, and the Superintendent of public schools had suspended classes for their students. The lines to get into the viewings were blocks long. Students, parents, community leaders, and members of the public stood for hours just to offer their condolences to the grieving families.

The Mayor and elected officials, including our governor, attended most, if not all, the funerals. For two long weeks, all we did was grieve. I cannot recall a time before in my life when I was so physically exhausted and that every fiber of my body ached. As soon as my head hit the pillow, I was asleep. Yes, some of the dreams that came were disturbing, and so there were too many restless nights. I wondered how Bishop Harrington was holding up. Yes, he carried on, but I knew it was taking a toll on him. Bishop was aging right before my eyes. So many new lines appeared on his face. His facial expressions were very reserved, almost nonexistent. Yet every day he went to the chancery, he carried on with the work of the diocese. For my part, I could see gray hair where once it was a light brown. Indeed, this tragedy had dramatically changed all our lives.

The explosion itself was a result of a gas leak that was brought about by work the gas company had been doing in the neighborhood. I could not imagine the litigation that would follow. Yet none would bring a single life back, nor would it make burnt skin whole again or be a remedy for an artificial limb(s).

The children who had attended our school were now being bused to other Catholic elementary schools within the city limits.

As things began to get back to normal, or what we would now call normal, the decision was made that the 150th anniversary/jubilee would be rescheduled for mid-October. Although late in the year, it would still be in our anniversary year and before all the fall and winter holiday events began.

Bishop ordered that the rest of the school building that was not destroyed by the explosion or fire be torn down. He did not want it standing one day longer than was necessary. It was presently a reminder of what tragedy took place on this property. A new school would be built on the land. It was also decided by the diocesan consultors that a permeant memorial be part of the new building so generations of future students and staff would never forget those who died or were injured that day.

In three weeks' time, Lou and Sharon will be united in the Sacrament of Marriage. It was going to be a simple Liturgy and reception. The two of them did not have the money for a large or elaborate wedding and reception. Since they were paying for all of it, they set a budget they could live with and were holding firm to it. They had invited fifty individuals to attend the reception and not allowing either family to add more to the number they were given. I will be the celebrant of the Liturgy, and Bishop Harrington would be present and bestow the nuptial blessing on the couple.

The day of the wedding was perfect. The sun was out, yet it was not overly hot or humid. Since the Mass was being celebrated in Sharon's parish church, her pastor would concelebrate with me. Some of the parishioners of Lou's former church came down to show their support of Lou and his decision. Most still called him Father Lou, and he would correct them that it was just Lou now or Mr. Lou Santiago. Sharon wore this simple white wedding dress that she found in one of the local boutique shops and looked stunning in it. Lou had rented a formal black tuxedo for himself and his brother who was his best man. As the two of them were processing out of the church, I thought to myself here is one of the few people that I know who will have received all seven sacraments of the Catholic Church. The reception was a buffet style, which kept the expense down for the two of them. They had a disc jockey who provided the music for dancing. I was fortunate to be able to dance twice with Sharon before the evening was over. Naturally, my mother was there for the wedding ceremony and reception. I knew she was a little sad seeing Lou married and no longer in active ministry. I think, somewhere in the back of her mother's mind, she was asking herself if Lou could fall in love like this, what about me, her son. So before Mom asked the question, while we were dancing, I whispered in her ear that I was not leaving, that I did not have a love interest outside the ministry I was engaged in. She looked at me and then said, "Now, what made you ever say something like that? It would never have crossed my mind." As soon as she uttered those words, we both broke into laughter knowing well that is exactly what was going on in my mom's head as we danced.

The chairman of the moral department at the seminary was going to be off giving a series of talks in Canada, and the rector had called and asked if it would be possible for me to fill in for him while he was gone. I assured the rector that I would love to do it, but was not sure if Bishop would be willing to let me go on short notice. During dinner that evening, I asked Bishop Harrington what he thought of me taking a week off, the week after next, to fill in for my former boss, Father Larry.

Bishop asked were there any events that I thought Father Peter would not be capable of handling during the time I was away? Having already looked at the calendar, I knew it was all pretty standard. Plus, I had taken the liberty of checking with Peter ahead of time to be sure he could do it if Bishop agreed. I only told Bishop that he would mainly be visiting local parishes, celebrating Mass with the people during my absence and that Father Peter was both capable of handling those, and he was also available at times they were scheduled.

Bishop Harrington just sat there, like he was giving this real thought before he smiled at me and told me to let the Rector know he was delighted to have me fill in for Father Larry, but not to get any ideas of having me full-time on the faculty again. At this time in history, Bishop wanted me here with him, and that was not open to discussion. I thanked him and assured Bishop that I was delighted doing what I was as his secretary and master of ceremonies.

Over the next week, I refreshed myself on the material I would be teaching. This time, it would just be with the fourth-year seminarians who were taking the course on Human Sexuality. When I was on the faculty, years ago, the Rector and I team-taught that course. The seminarians at that time never called it human sexuality among themselves; rather they called the course "Sex with the Rector and Friend." Although we were not supposed to know they called it that, in a confined community like the seminary, there really are no secrets. Over these last few years, with just Larry teaching it, everyone was back calling it the course on human sexuality again.

The week I would be there they would be looking at adolescent sexuality and the questions of masturbation, premarital intercourse, sexually transmitted diseases, gay, lesbian, and transgender relationships. As I got back into preparing for those topics, the juices ran through my veins again. There were times

I really missed teaching in the seminary. You were working with faculty members all chosen because they were some of the best in their fields. They were solid academic individuals who wanted to make sure the men they were instructing were well equipped to handle what they would be confronted within their ministry. But also, that they would be stepped in the rich tradition of the Catholic Church's history and teachings. It was an awesome responsibility, which I found every man teaching took seriously.

In a month from now, Bishop Harrington will ordain seven transitional deacons as priests for our diocese. It is always one of the highlights of the year for him. Before they were admitted to study for the diocese, each man went through a series of sessions with the therapists hired by the diocese to weed out those who had psychological issues, addictions, and whether they were comfortable with their sexuality. Seven men made it through and have proven to the faculty of the seminary that they are committed to being celibate priests who understand the need to lead a simpler life, be available to the poor and weak, and listened to the instructions of their bishop. I will be the official master of ceremonies, and Father Peter will give me a hand in making sure each man has what he needs.

Before their ordination, I still had to cover the moral classes for Father Larry. When Bishop walked me to my car the morning, I was leaving or the seminary he wished me well and told me how proud he was having me work for him. He also wanted me to take some time with one of the men to be ordained. Although the faculty had voted for his ordination, there had been some lively discussion about his fitness. The rector wrote that one faculty member stated that he knows his material, but I just have this feeling that the commitment to a lifetime of service is not there. I told Bishop that I would get him aside and talk with him and see what I could ascertain from his responses and demeanor.

I really got back in my academic groove and loved the give and take of the classroom. The men were articulate, intelligent, and thoughtful. Our diocese and the others represented in the class will be well served. In meeting with Charlie, the seminarian Bishop Harrington had asked me to check out, I found myself hearing a man say the right things, but there was no feeling behind what he said. Charlie knew his material, but I just could not put my finger on why I was uncomfortable with him. He would be a manly priest and a priestly man if ordained. Yet my gut said maybe he was not ready.

When I arrived back at the bishop's residence, I informed Bishop Harrington about my meeting with our man Charlie. I was blunt in that I could not find something outright that should hold up his ordination. However, like the one faculty member, I was not sure of his commitment to a life of service. I could offer no empirical proof, just an inner feeling that he was not telling me everything. Bishop thanked me and said he would pray over it and decide in the morning.

The next day, true to his word, Bishop called the rector of the seminary and informed him that he would not ordain Charlie at the end of May. He had also sent a letter telling Charlie of the same. Bishop suggested that Charlie take a pastoral leave of absence. He wanted Charlie to spend the next year in a parish, living with another priest(s) who lived their commitment out day after day. Bishop wanted him to see what it took to honestly be a priest. Naturally, his parents were upset with Bishop's decision as well as the pastor of the parish Charlie grew up in.

It rained the two days before the Ordination to the Priesthood. However, that Saturday morning it could not have been nice out. The procession from the Cathedral sacristy to the front doors took about five minutes because of the number of priests concelebrating. During the Mass, the Vicar-General calls each man up who is to be ordained. The Vicar-General will attest to their fitness to serve the diocese, and the people show their consent by the applause they give. Bishop led the Litany of the Saints as the seven men prostrated down the center aisle of the cathedral. The people invoked those holy men and women who have gone before us to invoke God's blessing on these men and make them good ministers of God.

The ordained deacons went one by one up to Bishop Harrington, placed their hands in his, and promised him and his successor's obedience and respect. Next, they have their hands anointed, presented with the sacred vessels and final the laying on of hands, first by the bishop and then by all the priests present. The newly ordained than concelebrated their first Eucharistic Liturgy with Bishop and all the other concelebrants. Finally, Bishop Harrington blessed the congregation and knelt down, and each new priest came forward and gave their first blessing to their ordaining bishop. After the Mass, the new priests went back into the cathedral and gave their blessing to their family, friends, and all who approached them. It was a joyous day for our diocese. After the two-and-a-half-hour Liturgy, Bishop and I went back to the residence so he could shower and change clothing. Bishop Harrington took a long-needed nap and slept like a child.

Shortly after I arrived at the chancery on Monday, my phone rang. When I answered, I heard the familiar voice of Detective Lieutenant James Teeling at the other end. He told me he saw the pictures of the ordination mass in the Sunday paper and we all seemed so happy in them. I assured him that it had been a beautiful day and wonderful celebration. Jimmy then told me they might know who the third person is in our case. The partial print the FBI was fairly sure belonged to Howard R. Thornton. Mr. Thornton had been arrested and served time for attempted murder in the past. He also had been a sharpshooter when he was in the Marines. Apparently, from his military record, an excellent one at that. They believed he was more than capable of having fired the shot from the cemetery, considering the distance involved and had it not been for the movement of the crozier a clean hit on Bishop. The problem Jimmy told me was they had no known address on the man. The last on record was in Arizona and having checked with the authorities there, it was determined he had not been in the state for at least two years. As a result, Teeling said, we may now know the possible third person, but we have no idea where he might be. Fortunately, a photo from the day he was released from prison has been distributed. However, in the ensuing years, he could easily have had plastic surgery or merely disguised himself so that he did not resemble the man in the picture. I asked if he could send a picture over to us, and he said it would be faxed to my office this morning by his secretary. I could at least make copies so our two security guards had some idea of what he could look like; plus, I would make sure

Bishop saw it as well. Thanking Jimmy for staying on top of this case, I hung up.

Two weeks have passed since the ordination of the new priests for the diocese. Today, Bishop received a call informing us that Charlie Hastings, the deacon Bishop told would have to spend a year on a pastoral leave and help out in an assigned parish, over the weekend was married. Not only was he married while still an ordained deacon, but he married a religious woman who was still active in her community. Apparently, neither had been dispensed. Bishop was not only shocked and angry but also thankful that he had not ordained him as priest. He asked me to draft a letter informing Charlies that the Church did not consider his marriage to be sacramental, although legal. All support from the diocese ceased as of this date. If he wanted to apply for laicization, he should contact my office, and I would forward the request and paperwork to Bishop Harrington. Since the diocese had paid for his education in the seminary, we would hold onto the insurance policy that was taken out on him to be cashed in when he died. Bishop also wanted me to express how disappointed he was that Deacon Hastings did not have the courtesy of informing Bishop himself of the marriage or the intention to marry. It was evident to all that their relationship had been going on while he was an ordained deacon and maybe even longer than that period of time.

I drafted two copies, one a little stronger than the other. Had Rose prepare both for Bishop. Ultimately he signed the one that was not as strongly worded or showed the anger Bishop felt at the moment. It went out in the afternoon mail. We did not believe that it would have any impact on the newly married couple, but it still had to be sent. Charles Hastings personnel file here at the chancery was flagged so any future Bishop would be made aware of the situation.

When we were home that evening and having dinner that Sister Anesia had prepared for us, she came in telling Bishop that Sister Kunegunda seemed to be tired of late and had already gone to bed. Right away, Bishop asked if she had seen her doctor. Sister Anesia told us they both did not think it was necessary. Probably just her age catching up. Sister Kunegunda was now in her late seventies. Bishop and I reminded Sister Anesia that if there was anything we could do, let either one of us know, and we would take care of it for them.

The next couple of weeks were business as usual. Each day we went to the chancery, came home, or went to a parish for an evening Liturgy, a local celebration or civic event. The city was emotionally coming back after the explosion at our elementary school, the deaths, and funerals. I knew that the firemen and police who were first at the scene were also seeing therapists provided by their unions. Death is one thing that can be difficult to deal with, but when it is little children, it is almost devastating on the psychic spirit. Our own group of inner-city priests had met for a total of eight times before we felt we were capable of processing all we said and heard that horrendous day.

It is now midsummer and the days are getting hotter and more humid each passing day. The chancery air-conditioning system was having a difficult time keeping up with the demand placed upon it. One factor is the fact that the system is sixteen years old. By today's standards not energy efficient or cost effective. It is on a list of major repairs, upgrades that have to be made here at the chancery. However, it is not scheduled for this year. Depending on the Fall and Winter fund drive for the diocese it may not be on next year's list either. Every year it is a balancing act that the finance committee has to do with what comes in and what the needs of the agencies are.

One significant expense will be the rebuilding of a new elementary school to replace the one that was destroyed. That will be a two-year, or less, project for the diocese and the superintendent's office. Plus, we also have the start of construction of the new building Mr. Martin Thompson gave us the financial gift for months ago.

The Office of Buildings and Properties had purchased a parcel of land, that adjoined the land the former school was on, and that will be sufficient to accommodate the type of facility he had envisioned. Matter of fact, he loved the architect's drawings of the proposed buildings. It was just last week that the City Council and Planning Board gave their approval for it to be built. We believe that the site is in an excellent area to draw many of our at-risk youth to it. Most will be able to walk there or take a short bus ride to the facility. Bishop decided, over the objection of Mr. Thompson, that it will be known as the "Thompson Learning and Recreation Center." The diocese had never received a single donation as large as the one Martin had bestowed upon it. Instead of naming it after a saint, Bishop felt that generations to come should know of Mr. Thompson's desire to see the youth of the city have a safe haven for food, after-school learning, and recreation.

The official groundbreaking will take place in two weeks now that all applications have been approved. Bishop will preside and bless the land the new center will rest on. We expect the Mayor, district representatives, as well as Mr. Thompson and the five other donors who stepped up after hearing about the donation made for such a center to all, have shovels in hand to turn over the first shovels of dirt. There is speculation that because of the scope of the facility that even the Governor will come down from the state house to participate in the ceremony. It will be a good day for our diocese and for the inner city as a whole. Since who may belong is not restricted to just Catholic children but to anyone who registers, it was a key factor in the city council's decision to approve it as well as the additional donors. They gave a total of twenty million. So we had thirty-five million to create these new facilities. The reality is these buildings will be a boost to the economy of the city as they are constructed and provide all the youth with a real alternative to just hanging around on the streets and possibly getting in trouble. It is a real solution where everyone benefits for the city, the church, and our youth.

Chapter 12

Thursday of this week, while working at my desk in the chancery, I heard the city's fire siren go off and then what seemed to be the sound of endless fire trucks and ambulances sirens blaring. Naturally, I hoped we were not dealing with another major tragedy in this great city of ours.

We did not receive any calls or notices that it was one of our buildings that were on fire. I turned the radio onto hear if anything was being announced over our local station. Within minutes of starting to listen the radio announcer said, "Repeating our earlier announcement, the Cathedral of St. John the Divine on Fourth and Lexington Streets is on fire. It is a major fire, and we understand that over one hundred firemen are fighting it and trying to protect nearby buildings. More news later in the broadcast."

I went down the hall to Bishop's office, after having checked with Rose that there was no one inside with him, knocked and entered. Bishop looked up from his desk and the papers he was signing. I informed him of what I had just heard over the radio. Instantly, he buzzed Rose to come in. When she appeared at the other doorway leading into his office, he asked her if we had Bishop Wallis's cell phone number. He was the Episcopal bishop, and it was their cathedral that was burning. Rose came back and told Bishop that we did not, only his office number. Bishop asked Rose to call there and ask the secretary to have Bishop Wallis call when he could. Bishop had Rose give Wallis's secretary his cell phone number.

Then Bishop picked up the phone and hit an auto dial number on it. The secretary of our cathedral rectory picked up after the first ring. Bishop announced it was himself and he wanted to talk immediately with Msgr. William Daley, rector of the cathedral. The secretary told Bishop that he was outside, but she would go get him and have him call back.

I looked at Bishop and asked what he had in mind? He smiled and told me he thought I would have already guessed what he intended. Looking somewhat puzzled back at him, I said I really did not know. Bishop Harrington began to tell me when his phone rang. He picked it up, and Msgr. Daley was on the other end. Immediately, Bishop informed Bill of his intention of making our cathedral available to the Episcopal Bishop for the duration of their repair. Bishop said he understood it would mean some significant changes in the time's masses were scheduled now, weddings and other events that were already in place. Msgr. Bill assured Bishop if that were his wish it would be done. Bishop thanked him and said that Bishop Wallis might not accept the gesture, but he wanted to offer our cathedral and did not want the staff at the rectory to be caught off guard if the gesture was taken. Bill said that he understood and would wait for further word. While waiting, he informed Bishop Harrington, he would see how they could rearrange scheduled masses and events to clear times for the Episcopal congregation to celebrate in our cathedral.

When Bishop hung up, I told him that now I understood. He said to me, "John, if you are ever a bishop, always remember that we are all God's sons and daughters. If one suffers, we all suffer. If you can do something for one of your brothers or sisters, do it in the name of the Lord, Jesus." I just shook my head that I understood and went back to my office.

The Episcopal Bishop called Bishop Harrington as Fred was driving us back home. He told Bishop that it looked like they had lost the entire sanctuary area of the cathedral. The fire apparently started in the sacristy and rapidly spread to the sanctuary.

Naturally, the rest of the cathedral suffered smoke and water damage. Bishop Harrington then offered the use of our cathedral, starting this weekend, if Bishop Wallis had no place to celebrate. I believe Bishop Wallis was both shocked and taken by the generous offer. He said he needed a day or so to get his mind clear of all that had happened, whether he could find one of his churches that could accommodate the cathedral congregation and would get back to Bishop Harrington as soon as he could. He asked Bishop why he was doing this and our Bishop only said, "Henry, we both serve the same God, the same Lord and Savior, it is what brothers should do for each other." Bishop Wallis said he understood and thanked Bishop for being the first to offer such relief and a reminder of our shared mission. I was pretty proud to be sitting next to this man and seeing the gospel not only preached but being lived out in real time.

When we arrived home, we both went to our respective rooms to get cleaned up for dinner. I walked through my office toward the bedroom and adjoining bathroom. I saw first the pile of my laundered clothing on top of the bed, so I knew Sister Kunegunda had already been there. Then my eye moved toward my bathroom, and instantly I saw her shoes. I ran over, and there lying on the floor was Sister Kunegunda. I reached down, touched her, and realized she was already dead. Her body was still warm, so I immediately grabbed the Oil of the Sick and anointed her. I then went down the hall and informed Bishop of her death. Immediately, Bishop Harrington went to my room and back to the bathroom and prayed over the body of Sister Kunegunda. Next, we called Harry Johnson, our local funeral director, and informed him and asked that he pick up the body. He told us to call her doctor and have her officially declared dead since the body was still warm. We did that and then went downstairs to inform her companion and friend, Sister Anesia of her death. Immediately Sister Anesia's eyes filled with tears and said she wanted to see her. We all went back upstairs, and she just knelt down and cradled the head of her beloved friend and fellow sister in religion. Sr. Anesia just rocked her as the tears ran down her face. As she was holding her, the doorbell rang and I ran downstairs to answer it. Doctor Mulligan was standing there, and I took him up to the body. He saw Sister Anesia holding her friend, and he knelt down next to her, listened for a heartbeat, and felt for a pulse, but neither existed. He then just put his arm around Sister Anesia and held her as she held Sister Kunegunda. *Why had I not thought of doing that?* I wondered. When the tears stopped, Doctor Mulligan released Sister Anesia and asked her to allow him to check her out. We both stepped out of the bathroom, and he checked her heart and pulse. Both were racing. He said he would prescribe a medication that would help her relax and take the pressure off of her heart. He knows it was a shock to Sr. Anesia and because of her age, he wanted to make sure he was not going to be called back again. I told him I would go and get the prescription. Just then, the doorbell rang again, and I went down to let Harry Johnson in. He had a stretcher and black bag with him and one assistant. I told him that Dr. Mulligan was still upstairs and would give him the official death certificate.

Doctor Mulligan brought Sister Anesia to her room. She said she had to serve dinner, and he told her not tonight. We were two grown men who could take care of ourselves and her this evening. He wanted her to rest and take the medication he was ordering after she ate something. As we were leaving her room, Harry and his assistant were bringing the body of Sister Kunegunda down the stairs on the stretcher. Now, all we saw was the black zipped bag that held the earthly remains of our friend. Bishop told Harry that he would cover all expenses involved in the preparation of her body, the coffin and whatever else there was involved. Bishop also said to him that her body should be waked in the church down the street and he would call the pastor and let him know. Our sisters, besides knowing the housekeeper Mary Jacoby, went there for Sunday Liturgies. Morning mass they could celebrate here with us, but since Bishop spent most weekends visiting parishes, the sisters always went down the street for Mass.

They would also visit the rectory after the Mass and have a cup of coffee and piece of pastry with Mary before returning to our residency. We knew Mary Jacoby would take the death of her friend hard, and we were correct.

Before we ate, and while I ran to the pharmacy to pick up the medication, Bishop Harrington called the Motherhouse of the Sisters of the Cross and asked for Mother Veronica, OC. When Mother got on, Bishop informed her of Sister Kunegunda's death. She was surprised and truly saddened by the news. She assured Bishop that she and her council members would be flying up for the funeral to be supportive of Sister Anesia. Bishop told Mother that he would want them to stay here with us and that we had sufficient room to accommodate her and how many council members would be coming. She thanked Bishop for the gracious offer and told him that they would indeed take him up on his offer.

Bishop went back to see Sister Anesia and tell her that Mother Veronica and some of the council would be coming to the funeral. Sister thanked Bishop for calling Mother and letting her know. Bishop also told her that they would all be staying here for the time of the wake and funeral to give support to her. Again, Sister thanked Bishop for arranging that.

Just as he was coming out of her room, I arrived back with her medication. The instructions said they were to be taken with food and that she was to take one a day starting tonight. So the two of us went into the kitchen. Sister Anesia already had stew cooking in a large pot on the stove. She had prepared biscuits, and they were ready to go into the oven. Rather than bother her, I called my mom and asked her how long I had to cook them and at what temperature. Before she answered, she questioned why I would be cooking biscuits while Sister Anesia was at home. I told her how we found Sister Kunegunda dead when we came back this evening and how I had to get some food into Sister so she could take her medication. Naturally, Mom said she would be right over, but I assured her that Sister already had the whole meal done, all we had to do was back the biscuits and serve the meal. My dear mother then told me to tell Bishop that she would be there the days of the wake and funeral so that Sister Anesia would not be obliged to cook. And she made sure I understood that she would not take no for an answer. When I hung up and told Bishop, he just laughed and said how grateful he was for my mom.

I baked the biscuits, and when they were ready, we set three places at the table. Bishop went and brought Sister Anesia to the table and had her sit and eat with us. After Bishop had prayed the prayer of thanksgiving for this food and the life of Sr. Kunegunda, we all sat to eat. Hardly a word was spoken throughout the meal. Each of us absorbing what had taken place. We knew that Sister Kunegunda might not be replaced by the Motherhouse. There was also the possibility that Sr. Anesia would be brought back to live at the Motherhouse since the community did not allow any sister to live on her own. Each house had to have a minimum of at least two sisters living in it. We did tell Sister Anesia that my mother Gert, would be here for the days that Sister Veronica and the council members were in the house. She protested and said she was capable of cooking. However, Bishop interjected that he would appreciate her allowing my mother to do it so she could be free to go to the wake and funeral without worrying about preparing food for all of us. Reluctantly, Sister agreed but let us know it was her job. Bishop assured her that it was her job for as long as she wished, knowing that the decision might not be in her hands but in the hands of her superior.

After dinner, Bishop and I cleaned up, put the leftovers in the refrigerator, gave Sister her medication, and went to our respective rooms. I put my clothes away that Sister Kunegunda had left on my bed.

Bishop received a call on his cell phone from Bishop Wallis telling him that he would accept the gracious offer of using our cathedral until the repairs could be done on their building. Bishop asked him to make all the arrangements with Msgr. William Daley, whom Bishop would have call Bishop Wallis tomorrow morning. Bishop then placed the call to Bill at the cathedral and told him to call Bishop Wallis and arrange the times they would like to use our cathedral.

Early the next morning, after we had celebrated Mass and had breakfast, Bishop received a call from Mother Veronica saying they would arrive at our airport on Thursday afternoon at three twenty. Bishop told her that he would send Mr. McNamara to pick them up and bring them to the residence. Bishop gave me the news and told me to call Mr. Harry Johnson and find out when Sister Kunegunda's body would be ready.

When we arrived at the chancery, the first thing I did was call Harry Johnson and ask him when he expected to have the body ready. He told me that he would be working on her today and if I could please bring over a clean habit for her to be laid out in he would appreciate it. I called the house and asked Sister Anesia if she would get a clean habit of Sister Kunegunda's, and I would be over in about a half hour to pick it up and bring it to the funeral home. Sister said she would have their formal habit ready for my pickup. Most of the time, in the residence they wore a simple white habit and veil to work in. I brought over her good white habit, the dark red tunic with a white cowl attached and gave them to Harry.

Harry told me they intended to bring her body over to the church at 2:00 PM on Friday and wanted to know who would accept it. I told him that Father Thomas the pastor and Bishop along with the Superior General of the Order would be present to receive the body and walk it to the front of the church. The coffin Harry said would be then be opened as requested. I thanked him and assured him that Father Thomas and I would take care of all the liturgical things that needed to be there.

I then went back to the chancery to finish up on business there. On my desk, in today's mail, was a letter from Charlie Hastings, our now married deacon. In the letter, he informed he had no intention of playing the silly games of the Roman Catholic Church and asking to be laicized by Rome. Whether we considered his marriage to be valid was of no consequence to him or his wife, the former Sister Mary Elizabeth. He told me that he did not want to hear from Bishop or anyone else in the chancery from this point forward. I took the letter down to Bishop who was surprised by the content and tone. He asked that I put it into his personnel file and be done with the matter. I did exactly what Bishop asked me to do and brought this matter to a close.

This afternoon, Fred went to the airport to pick up Mother Mary Veronica, OC, and two members of her council. As a result, I drove Bishop to work today and now am driving him back to the house. We want to be there when the sisters arrive to greet and welcome them to Bishop's residence.

When we got home, Sister Anesia greeted us at the door in her formal habit. My mom had already arrived and was busy in the kitchen. Sister had taken the time to show her where a few things were that my mother could not locate when she filled in for the sisters. Apparently, the two of them hit it off right from the start. Bishop had called my mother, unknown to me, and asked if it was okay with her that she cook for six each time. Mother, being a mother, told him it was not an issue. That when you raise a family as large as ours, she was used to cooking for that number. Bishop thanked her and last night told Sister Anesia that she, Mother, and the councilors would be joining us for meals while they were here for the wake and funeral.

We had only been home about thirty minutes when Fred called on his cell phone to let us know he was about ten minutes away.

I went down to Bishop's rooms and found him in his office going over some correspondence. As soon as he heard the news, he was up from the desk chair and on his way downstairs. He looked around the sitting room to make sure everything was in order. He took a bottle of wine from the small refrigerator and put it on the serving tray. He actually seemed a little anxious, flustered, I am not sure what or why. I looked at Bishop and told him that everything looked fine. He then said to me that whenever he had to deal with Major Superiors of the Orders that worked in the diocese, he got nervous. He never knew what they were going to ask or want. I reminded him that they were here for Sister Kunegunda's funeral. "Ah," Bishop said, "and she will also be telling us if she wants Sister Anesia to go back with her and that they are no longer going to providesSisters to take care of the house and us." I was naive in thinking this was just about the funeral. Bishop knew from years of experience that nothing was ever as they seemed in situations like this.

When Fred opened the front door of the residence, I was surprised at what I saw. Behind him were three religious women all in the habit of the Sisters of the Cross. Two were probably in their late fifties or early sixties. The other tall woman was probably in her early forties. I would quickly learn, as they introduced themselves to us, that the two older sisters were the council members accompanying their superior. Sister Veronica, Mother General, stood as tall as our Bishop. She was an incredibly attractive woman, even in full habit. Her face was very smooth, vibrant blue eyes that captivated you. Yet there was something that said she was a person you knew you did not want to tangle with or get on her bad side.

The first thing Mother Veronica did was go over and embrace Sister Anesia. Sr. Anesia started to cry, and Mother just held her and told her that she would take care of her and that was why they were here. She knew how close the two of them had been and how painful this had to be for her. Sister Anesia just shook her head in agreement. Mother gave her a gentle kiss on the check and only then did the two other sisters come over and embrace Sr. Anesia. I did learn that the shorter and oldest was Sr. Mary Angela, and the other was Sr. Mary Louise.

Bishop offered us all a glass of wine, but the sisters declined and asked, if Bishop did not mind, they would like to spend a little time just with Sister Anesia? Bishop naturally agreed, and Sr. Anesia said they could go to the sitting room the two sisters used and was next to their bedrooms.

When they left the room, Bishop asked, "Did I see those eyes on Mother Veronica?" I laughed and told him that I would not want to have to play hardball with her. He had also noted, even though Mother seemed young for her position, she immediately showed that her concern and care was for Sr. Anesia. He thought that was a good sign, where I had seen it as a sign that she would be taking her back with them. In two days from now, we will know, one way or the other.

I told Bishop I was going to the kitchen to see if my mother needed any help. Naturally, Mom did not need any. She was in her element. Everything smelled so good. Mother had roasted a pork loin and was going to serve with mashed potatoes, gravy, green beans with almond, and glazed carrots. She had prepared a large bowl of salad and told me to put that on the table. The dressings were already on our dining table I saw when I placed the bowl of salad there. Mom had also baked at home and brought it with her, a homemade pumpkin pie, and that was for dessert. I saw she had both coffee and tea not knowing what the sisters drank available for them. She knew that Bishop and I would be having coffee.

At six, my mom rang the dinner bell, and we all gathered around the table. Bishop Harrington said the blessing and all sat down. I went to the kitchen and assisted my mother in bringing all the food to the table. Bishop proceeded to introduce my mother to Sister Veronica and Sisters Mary Angela and Louise.

They were so thrilled to be able to meet my mom, and she just beamed. The two council members told Gert how Sister Anesia said I was not only a good priest but a good boy also, always asking her if there was some way he could be of help. I was embarrassed to know she spoke of me and that she saw me as a boy. I was in my early forties, but if you are in your seventies, I guess I was a boy to her.

Dinner conversation revolved around stories of Sister Kunegunda. The older Sister, Mary Angela, had been training to be a Sister of the Cross just as Sr. Kunegunda was in her last year of the novitiate. So she had known her or worked with her over the ensuing years. We all seemed to have a tale to two to share, and there were much laughter and good remembrances. During the meal, and in between stories, Bishop told the sisters when the body would be brought to the church and how he and the pastor would like Sr. Veronica to join him in welcoming the body to the church tomorrow. She thanked him and told Bishop she would like that very much. Since she was the elected Mother General of their Order, in her person rested the values and connection to all the other 352 religious women who at present were members of the Sisters of the Cross.

As we got up from dinner, the sisters told us they would be going back with Sr. Anesia until it was time for them to retire. They asked what time

Bishop celebrated Mass in the morning and he told them at six thirty. They assured him they would all be up and attending. I went and gave my mother a hand cleaning up the kitchen and doing the dishes. When everything was spotless Mom said she would be going home but would be back in time to make us breakfast. She would stay to handle lunch for all the sisters and naturally prepare our evening meal again. I walked her to her car and gave her a kiss. She told me how much she loved me and how proud she was of me.

The next day, after Mass and breakfast, Bishop informed the sisters he had to go to the chancery and that he and I would see them when the body arrived. Also, that Fred would be available to drive them anywhere they would like. Since the Order has three sisters working at one of our parishes, Sister Veronica said that she and her council members would like to pay them a visit. She wanted some private time with them and knew that the funeral would not afford them time to spend with those sisters.

Chapter 13

At one thirty, Fred drove Bishop and me over to St. Augustine Church to receive the body of Sr. Mary Kunegunda, OC. Upon arriving at the Church, we went into the sacristy, and Bishop changed clothing. After putting on his alb, cincture, and stole, I placed the pectoral cross around his neck and the white cope around his shoulders. Father Thomas, the pastor and I both just wore an alb and stole. When we came out of the sacristy, Bishop saw that the sisters were already in the church, plus a good number of parishioners. Father Tom and I followed the cross bearer and two acolytes, and Bishop invited Sr. Mary Veronica, OC, to walk alongside him to greet her deceased sister in religion.

The funeral director had arranged to have his staff help carry the body inside the church and place it on the carriage. Bishop began the prayers and then asked Sr. Veronica to take the one that formally welcomed Sister's body into the church for viewing. When we all processed to the front of the church and the carriage was placed in its proper position with the head facing the altar, the director and one assistant removed the top of the coffin. The assistant took it and put it in the sacristy. Mother Veronica then went and put a crown of roses on Sr. Kunegunda's head before she pulled the cowl over her face as was their custom. Bishop blessed the body with Holy Water, and we departed. Mother Veronica had Sr. Anesia stand next to her and then Sr. Angela and Louise joined them.

All four greeted and thanked the parishioners who had gathered to be the first for this wake. Ms. Mary Jacoby came up, touched the hands of her friend, and went over and embraced Sister Anesia. Both cried as they held one another. Sr. Anesia introduced Mary to her general superior and two councilors. They thanked Mary for being such a good and dear friend to both of the sisters. Mary told them that she would miss Sister Kunegunda. Mother Veronica just bent down and kissed Mary on the cheek and said, "I know you will."

That evening, I and Father Tom conducted the actual wake service. The parish choir volunteered to come that night and sing for the wake. I knew they would be back tomorrow morning to sing for the funeral Mass but had not expected them this evening. It seems, unknown to us, after all these years the two sisters had made quite a few friends of those who attended that early Sunday Liturgy.

The next day was the funeral. I was delighted to see there were about one hundred people gathered to celebrate the Mass with us. The three other Order of the Cross Sisters serving in our diocese were present. After the Liturgy, her body was taken to the cemetery attached to the parish grounds. At the grave site, both Bishop and Mother Veronica prayed that God receives His daughter back into the Kingdom of God.

Gert had a meal prepared for all of us when we arrived back home. During the meal, Sister Veronica asked Bishop if she could speak with him privately after the meal. Naturally, he agreed, but I did notice that after saying that he just picked at his food. I know he was worried that Mother Veronica was going to tell him that Sister Anesia would be going back with them to South Carolina and to the Motherhouse.

When we finished, Bishop and Sister Veronica went into the sitting room where they could be alone. Not wasting any time, Mother looked Bishop in the eyes and said that she had discussed with Sr. Anesia her present situation now that Sister Kunegunda was deceased. Because Mother Veronica had met privately with each of them while they vacationed at the motherhouse she was well aware of what each sister meant to the other and how they felt about the work they were doing here with us. Mother asked Sister Anesia if she wanted to come home to the motherhouse when they met with her yesterday. Sr. Anesia said she enjoyed her work here but knew that their policy was that no sister live and work alone. So if Mother wanted her back, she would go. Mother Veronica and the two members of her council told Sister Anesia that is what they thought she would say. Then, Mother asked her, if she would be comfortable with Sister Agnes Gregory coming to be the new housekeeper. Sister Anesia and Sister Agnes have known each other for ages. Sr. Agnes Gregory has been in charge of the communications department of the Order and was about to retire early. She had agreed to this new position if, and only if, Sister Anesia, agreed. Sister Anesia was over-joyed. And so, Sister Veronica told Bishop that not only would Sister Anesia be staying but that Sister Agnes Gregory would be joining her. Mother had been so impressed by Bishop's kind Christmas gift and gesture of the two weeks' vacation back to the Motherhouse that she said she just could not stop this ministry if she had sisters available and willing. She also told Bishop that Sister Agnes Gregory, OC, would arrive on Thursday of the coming week if that was all right with him. Bishop Harrington was overjoyed by the news that not only were they not leaving, but a new housekeeper would be here this very week. He told Mother that would be okay and he would have Fred pick her up at the airport. Mother Veronica thanked Bishop again for being so kind to her sisters and looked forward to years of working with the diocese.

That evening, Fred took the three sisters back to the airport for their trip home to South Carolina.

On Monday, Bishop and I were both back to work in the chancery. Bishop wanted to check with Msgr. Bill Daley if he had called Bishop Wallis. Bill told Bishop that they had been able to work out a schedule for the use of our cathedral. Msgr. said he was sure that Bishop Wallis would have liked to have greater use of our building, but the schedule of pre-planned events just allowed the days and times agreed upon. Bishop thanked him for doing his best to accommodate the Episcopal Bishop and congregation as they repaired their cathedral.

I called the diocesan chaplain for Boy Scouts to ascertain if everything was ready for this Saturday's distribution of religious scout awards to both the youth and their leaders. Father Ralph assured me that everything was in order and all Bishop would have to do is hand out awards. One of the county chaplains was going to be the speaker, so Bishop did not have to prepare a talk for them. Father Ralph asked if I was going to assist Bishop for Benediction of the Blessed Sacrament, or was he supposed to do that? I told him that I would be there and handle that part of the celebration. I asked him how many awards would be given out and he said there would be 180 of them. Most were going to the boys, but twenty were being awarded to the adult leaders. I said I would pass the information off to Bishop that evening. Bishop always looked forward to this and the Girl Scout award ceremony. He made sure that Rose always kept the dates clear on his calendar, so there was no problem with him presiding at the ceremonies.

I did let Detective Teeling know that we would once again be dealing with a large crowd of youth, their leaders, and parents. He told me to make sure Bishop was wearing his bulletproof vest. I assured Jimmy that Bishop was very faithful in wearing it. I asked if through the depositions that had been taken, did they find the reason Bishop was targeted by them to be killed? He said as far as he had heard from the prosecutor's office they had not identified a particular reason. They were looking into the diocese he had been bishop of before being sent to our diocese. They were trying to determine if any of these three people of interest lived, worked there, or had made any threats against the Church while he was the ordinary. I thanked him for keeping on to of this, and all the department was doing.

As promised, Sister Agnes Gregory, OC, arrived on her flight from South Carolina at 11:30 AM. Fred McNamara was there with a printed sign in his hands at the baggage claim area. Not that he really needed one since you do not see sisters in full habit coming into the area that often these days. Sister spotted the sign and went over and introduced herself to Fred. He told her if she gave him her baggage claim ticket he would wait at the carousel for her. So she did just that and handed the claim ticket over. Within minutes of the luggage appearing, he spotted her tag, grabbed the suitcase, and joined Sr. Agnes Gregory. Fred led her to the parking garage and to the diocesan car. He put her luggage in the trunk and opened the back door for her. Sister got in, and Fred ran around the other side, got in, and started the drive back to the residence. The two of them chatted along the way. Sister wanted to know how long Fred had been driving the bishop. He told her for the five years he has been here but drove his predecessors for seventeen years before Bishop Harrington arrived. He was always anxious when a new bishop came in wondering if his services would still be needed. Fred was getting up in years and knew that one of these days, some Bishop would probably not want a driver but would either drive himself of have a priest assigned to him do it. He told her how his wife had died, and it had been difficult after that, but the job kept him grounded and a purpose for getting out of bed each day. Fred also told Sister Agnes how this year Bishop had him over for Christmas dinner with Sr. Kunegunda of happy memory, Sr. Anesia and Father John. Then he asked about her life.

Sister told him that almost her entire ministry had been in their development office and communication center. She produced their radio show tapes, took care of all publicity coming out of the Motherhouse and trained new sisters in communications. But it was time for some new blood, and she knew that it was time. Not sure what she was going to do, Mother only suggested that she might want to consider being sent here. She admitted she did not have much experience as a housekeeper. But she had been doing her laundry for more years than she could count, ironing, and cleaning her own room; as well as the communication center. Plus, she knew Sr. Anesia very well and was looking forward to being with her. Sr. Agnes Gregory would fill her in on what the late Sr. Kunegunda's daily routine was like, and she was sure she would be able to handle it.

By the time they arrived at the residence, our Fred knew a great deal more about Sr. Agnes Gregory, OC, than Bishop or me. We would learn much from Fred over the next few days as he drove us back and forth to the chancery.

I must say that Sr. Agnes was a breath of fresh air in the house. Talk about full of energy. She was like a little hurricane rushing through rooms, cleaning, doing laundry and helping Sr. Anesia in the kitchen. For a person who had not done a lot of domestic things during her previous ministry, she was fantastic. That first Saturday, Mary Jacoby, made sure she came over to meet the new sister. She also brought along a huge pan of her lasagna that Bishop loved. The three of them, I am told, sat for about an hour having tea and cookies just chatting away. Bishop and I were happy that Sr. Agnes Gregory fitted in so well.

Saturday afternoon we had the Annual Scout Award Ceremony. Father Bill, who was one of the country Boy Scout chaplains, was the assigned preacher this year. He did a marvelous job of showing how Lord Baden Powell, founder of the Boy Scouts, vision was being lived out in these young men and adult leaders. When he finished, Father Ralph, the diocesan chaplain began to read the names of those being awarded. Each scout came forward, genuflected, and Bishop then handed them their medal. It took over thirty-five minutes before he gave all the Ad Altare Dei Award, Pius XII, awards to the boys and the Bronze Pelican and St. George medals to the adults. We all then participated in Benediction of the Blessed Sacrament and processed out. Bishop stood at the entrance and greeted parents, friends, and scouts as they came out of the cathedral.

When we arrived back at the residence, Bishop said he was going to go up to his rooms and try to get some work done before retiring early. He found he was getting tired more frequently and did not have his usual level of energy. I suggested he see his primary physician and Bishop said he had already scheduled an appointment for a week from now. It would be at that checkup and the follow-up tests that would take place that Walter Harrington learned he had cancer. All those years of pipe smoking were now taking their toll on his body.

For just a brief second, I thought maybe Bishop will die of natural causes before he could be assassinated. I knew it was wrong to think that way, but I surely did not want him to be killed by some person holding a grudge against him or the Church.

The next week seemed to go by very quickly. Before I knew it, we were off to celebrate Mass on Saturday at one of the rural parish churches and the next day we would be in one of our suburban churches.

On Monday evening, I got a call on my cell phone. It was my mom who was crying, trying to tell me something, but it was hard to understand her as she kept crying. Finally, she was able to get out that my younger brother Victor was killed by a drunken driver on his way home from work today. The driver went through a red light and slammed right into the driver side of my brother's car. The police said he died instantly from the force of the impact. The drunken driver was being chased by the police when the accident occurred. They had tried to pull him over because they noticed the erratic driving. However, as soon as they put their lights and siren on, he took off like a bat out of hell. The officers pursued him for three blocks when he ran that light and collided with my brother's car, which spun around and hit another vehicle. Kathy, Victor's wife, was taken to the hospital by one of the patrol cars. Naturally, she called my mom and her mother. Kathy asked her mom to go to the house and take care of my three nephews until she got home. She had just told the boys he had been in an accident, and she was going to the hospital with this police-man. I asked where they all were. Mom said that she and Kathy were still with the mangled body of my brother. The hospital had given them just a few more minutes to be with his body before it was taken down to the morgue. They asked Kathy if she had a funeral director who would pick up the body. Kathy told them that she did not, that this was not supposed to happen. I told Mom that I would meet them at Vic and Kathy's house and I would call Harry Johnson the funeral director we used to go over and retrieve the body.

I did not change out of my clerical clothing, just grabbed my car keys, went down to let Bishop know what happened and was on my way to the house and the boys. I arrived about ten minutes after Kathy, and my mother had gotten there. Kathy had just informed the three boys that their daddy had been killed and would not be coming home.

When I walked into the house all you could hear was the crying. The boys were crying, their Mom who is trying to console them was crying, both grandmothers and one grandfather were all crying. As soon as the kids saw me, they ran over and grabbed onto me for dear life as if they were afraid I would be taken from them. Vic and I had many similar characteristics, and most people thought we looked alike. Having been born, just two minutes apart, I guess I understood it. In me, the boys saw their dad and were determined not to let go. After about five minutes they began to loosen their grip on my legs and waist and asked what was going to happen to Dad. I told them that whatever pain their daddy might have experienced is nothing like the joy he now shares in God's Kingdom and presence.

I tried to explain to them that when their mommy gave birth to each one of them, there was a period of intense pain, but the minute she heard them cry and a nurse handed them to her, it was replaced with an utter joy that she had given birth to a boy. But first, they had to pass from the comfort of Mommy's womb into the bright lights and noise of the delivery room. But that was the start of a whole new life for them. So now, Daddy has done the same thing. He has passed from something he has known and loved for something new and wondrous, and your daddy prepares a place for us when it is our turn to be where he is. The boys just said, "Uncle Jack, are you telling us that Dad is okay and with God now?" I looked at my three nephews and said that was exactly what I was trying to tell them, but probably had used too many words. My oldest nephew, Baron, looked at me and stated that "You always talk too much, especially when you're preaching."

Harry Johnson called on my cell phone and told me that he had picked up Vic's body but said it would take a few days to prepare it before the family could view him. Harry said he felt that they would be able to cover up most of the damage done to the face. I asked him to let me know when he thought we could hold the wake. He said that he would call a day or two ahead and let me know. It was that they had also picked up two other bodies today, and they would also need to be prepared. I understood completely.

I stayed till around 11:00 PM with my sister-in-law, Mom, and her parents. The boys had already gone to bed. I told Kathy I would be back tomorrow to check on the kids, and she was appreciative of that.

Bishop Harrington was waiting up for me to return. I was now able to fill him in on more of the details and how the family was holding up. He asked me how I was doing? I honestly responded that I was not sure. I thought I was still in shock. All our early life and teenage years we were inseparable. Vic constantly teased me about being the oldest in the family, even if it was only by those two minutes. After I was ordained and Vic married, we were not able to spend the quality time we used to do when single. Bishop patiently listened and then said to me he wanted me to take the next few days off.

"Be present to your mom and three nephews, as well as your sister-in-law. As soon as Harry Johnson, the funeral director lets you know when the wake and funeral Mass are going to take place, you let me know. I will be present for both. I am going to presume that you are going to be the principal celebrant of your brother's funeral Liturgy and will handle the wake service. However, if at any time, you feel you cannot you just give me a look, and I will take over for you. You're always at my side, John, let me now be by your side." I thanked him and said I needed to get to my room, pray, and try to sleep. Bishop embraced me and told me "Good night!"

Bishop made sure that the sisters had been informed. Sister Anesia was right there at my side as soon as I came down for breakfast. She hugged me and told me how lucky I had been to have such a great relationship with my brother. Sr. Agnes Gregory offered her condolences to me and said she would keep our family in her prayers. I thanked them both and just then Bishop entered the room for breakfast. The sisters went back to the kitchen, and after grace, we sat down. Bishop said I looked tired and I told him that I had not slept that well trying to get my head around my brother's death. I was not sure how Kathy and the boys were going to be able to maintain their home, the kids schooling and everything else. I knew that Kathy did not make enough to cover all the expenses. It would be one of the subjects our families would have to discuss with her. He reminded me again that if he could be of any help, he was there for the family and me.

Bishop left for the chancery at his usual time. I stayed in my room going over the Scriptures and which ones we might want to use for Victor's funeral. Hopefully, family members will be able to do the readings, but if not, I knew others who would step in. I really am not aware of the pastor of the church they attend. Made a note for me to give him a call and see what his thoughts were on the wake service and funeral.

When I finally had a chance to call Father Bob, the pastor of the parish Vic, Kathy, and the boys have always gone to, he was most gracious to me. He did ask if I was going to be the principal celebrant of the Eucharistic Liturgy and I told him I would be and that I would be preaching. He then asked since he had known them for many years if I would mind if he conducted the evening wake service at the funeral home? Frankly, I thought I would be doing it but realized that there is a bond between pastor and parishioner that needs to be acknowledged and respected. After all, Kathy and the boys will be going to the parish for many more years I hope. I told him that I thought his suggestion was an excellent idea and asked him to concelebrate the Mass with me and whatever priests attended. Since Victor was my brother, I was sure there would be a good turnout of our diocesan priests at the wake and the Liturgy.

When I arrived at my sister-in-law's house, everyone was already present. Kathy told me that she had gone that morning to their safety deposit box and taken out their will and insurance policies. The will was clear, everything went to the living spouse at the death of one of them. She did find one insurance policy that Victor apparently took out after their first son was born. It was in the amount of five million dollars. Kathy not only did not know about it, but she was also stunned. The money would take care of paying off the mortgage on the house, caring for all three of the boy's college educations and allow her to continue to raise them right here in the house they knew. The kids could keep going to the school they were comfortable attending and remain in the parish that had always been a source of joy for them. It meant that she would not have to deprive the boys of summer vacations or their annual ski trip.

Kathy's dad told her that he would call Kathy and Victor's solicitor as soon as they had copies of his death certificate. He would ask the lawyer to take care of making sure everyone who needed a death certificate received it and that the insurance company was notified of his death, the policy number and how to reach his office if there were any questions regarding the money being electronically placed in Kathy and Victor's joint checking account. Kathy thanked her dad and said if there were any documents she needed to sign that he should just bring them to her.

Later after Harry Johnson called to inform me that despite the damage that had been done by the accident, he was sure that what Kathy and the boys saw, would look like Vic was just sleeping. Their cosmetologist had worked marvels in filling in gashes and covering bruises that should have been obvious. Harry told me that he had talked with Father Bob and the wake was set for 7:30 PM and the Funeral Liturgy would be at ten o'clock on Saturday. Visiting hours would start Friday afternoon at two o'clock for the public. He did recommend that the immediate family come around twenty minutes ahead of time so we all could have some private time before the public was allowed in for the viewing. I thanked Harry and assured him that we would be there on time.

The wake seemed to go on forever. There were so many who came through we never really had a chance to sit down. I have no idea how many of my priest colleagues visited. People from Vic's workplace came in high numbers and told us how much he was respected and how kind and gentle of a person he had been. Bishop came around eight fifteen, after the wake service, which Father Bob made personal, informal, and uplifting. I hoped that the next morning, my homily would be as good. Before Bishop had Fred drive him and the sisters back, he told me that he had called Father Peter to be his master of ceremonies for the Liturgy. That meant that Peter would, in reality, be mine, since Bishop was only going to preside at it. I thanked him for thinking of that and knew that having Peter at my side, no liturgical errors would be made. When you are under stress, it is unbelievable how the littlest things you do without even thinking, now you cannot remember. Peter would always have the page turned to the correct place, a finger gently pointing to the prayer to be prayed, handing me the Holy Water and sprinkler, incense, and censer and gently touching my arm when I seemed to be moving in the wrong direction or forgetting something.

The next morning, we were all back at the funeral home for our final viewing and the closing of the coffin. As a family, we had decided that we all wanted to be there when Mr. Johnson lowered Vic's head pillow, pulled the small blanket up over his hands and chest, and bring the lid down and lock it in place. We knew that it might be difficult for the boys but felt that they should be aware that their daddy's body was shown the utmost respect and dignity before they would see it no more. I stood with the boys, and yes, they cried some, but they did not try and run away but now knew that when they saw his coffin in church, they would know exactly what their daddy was like inside of it. Over 125 priests of the diocese concelebrated the Mass. They filled over half the pews on one side of the church behind the pallbearers. Bishop joined me for the final commendations and blessed and incensed the body of my brother.

The parish did not have its own cemetery, so we had to drive to one owned by the diocese. There the final interment took place, and I conducted the short prayer service. Instead of going back to the house, we had rented the Knights of Columbus Hall and went there for a meal that was being prepared by the women of Victor and Kathy's parish. Father Bob had asked the Altar Rosary Society of which Kathy was a member if they would arrange the cooking and serving. They were delighted to have been invited and prepared a meal that fed all the priests that stayed, plus all our family and friends.

When I did arrive back at the residence that night, Bishop was waiting for me. He told me that I had done a great job and gave an excellent homily. Twice during it, I had gotten choked up, but Bishop insisted it showed how close Vic and I had been over the years. He also felt the large turnout of priests was a credit to me. Then he said something extraordinary. He put his hand on my shoulder and said, "John, learn from today. Today you saw how strong you can be, how much your brother priests respect you and that type of respect every Bishop needs if he is to be a good shepherd to the people." I did not understand why he made such a statement but thanked him for his kindness and always showing me how to be a better man and priest.

I would like to say that life went back to normal the next week. It did not. I was exhausted, my body ached, my thoughts were all over the place, and at the least unexpected moment, I would burst out in tears. I could be driving down the highway and just start crying. All the emotions that had been restrained or buried after Victor's death were now pouring out of me. I could only imagine what it was like for Kathy and the boys, or for my mom. We all would be hurting for some time after this tragedy. Time does not heal, it gives distance. What we lost remains a void in our life. We move on because we have no choice but to move on or go crazy with grief. The hole left in my heart, my psyche will always be there. We were brothers from birth. We were comrades in arms when playing war games in the backyard. We were the one the other turned to when words could not be spoken. That type of void does not heal with time, but time gives us the distance we need to see it in a different perspective.

One of the priests who attended the funeral was down here at the chancery today. He had an early meeting this afternoon with the Boss. I would learn that evening as we were driven back that Father David Bergger had been diagnosed with Parkinson's disease. He came to inform Bishop of the fact and that for now, he would like to continue the work that he was doing. Bishop assured him that as long as his health allowed that he would not put him on sick leave. Father David is bilingual and has worked with the Hispanic community for about half of his whole ministry.

Like most dioceses in the United States, our clergy is aging. Although Bishop ordained six new men, we have ten retiring and two going on sick leave. Father David will be the third if the disease should make it difficult for him to speak or control his limbs. We all can recall how St. John Paul II had given an example to the world of how to deal with the crippling disease when he struggled with his Parkinson's. In due time, Father Dave would find himself confronting the loss of his body. No longer will do as his brain commands. In some ways, you become a prisoner in your own body. Prescription medications can slow down the progression of the disease, but there is no cure for it. Father David told Bishop Harrington that he was already taking the drugs. Fortunately for him, he has a strong group of friends who will watch over him, and assist him in knowing when to let go of active ministry.

Bishop often would relate this quote of Dieter F. Uchtdorf:

> "The Church is not an automobile showroom—a place to put ourselves on display so that others can admire our spirituality, capacity, or prosperity. It is more like a service center. Where vehicles in-need of repair come for maintenance and rehabilitation."

Father David has the chance, in the next months, to show friends and foes alike, how one dies. How do we deal with the ravishes inflicted by a disease we did not want? He can become an example of complete dependence on God for the strength he needs just to get through the day. And when he can no longer take in air and gives up the spirit, he can restore hope in his friends in the resurrection of the dead. Bishop said that was his earnest hope for Father David Bergger.

Chapter 14

Once again, the 150th anniversary of the founding of the diocese is back on track in rescheduling the concert, jubilee mass, and formal dinner. The same committee that initially worked on it and planned all the events and organization is still in place and working hard. This week, the new invitations will go out. We will all be praying that nothing will interfere with this celebration this time around.

In two weeks' time, Bishop Harrington will be going to Philadelphia for the fall meeting of the United States bishops. Bishop was looking forward to the time with his colleagues.

Just before I was ready to leave my office in the chancery the phone rang and I answered. Detective Teeling was on the other end. They had traced the bullet and gun back to a Roger Trent. When questioned by the FBI field agents in Chicago, he informed them that he had sold it to a man by the name of Howard Thornton at the annual gun show held each year in Chicago. As of late this morning, a bulletin went out looking for Howard Thornton as our prime suspect in the attempted murder of Bishop. Jimmy Teeling also told me they found out from Bishop's former diocese that at least once they had received death threats against the Church. At that time, no one person was mentioned. Records showed that Howard Thornton was living in Chicago at the time. His father had been denied burial by the local pastor because he was not a registered member of the parish. The Thornton family had written Bishop Harrington and asked him to allow the funeral to take place at their local church. Bishop, according to a copy of his letter in the file, had refused to overrule the local pastor. The FBI and our police department now had the links they were seeking. The last piece of the puzzle was the whereabouts of one Howard Thornton. No federal tax return had been made by him, nor could a driver license be established. The last one on record had expired four years ago, and that was issued by the State of Illinois. I commented to Det. Teeling that his department and the whole law enforcement body had done a great job so far and hoped that shortly they would have in custody Howard Thornton and charges pressed against all three. Jimmy assured me that was their desire and objective. Once again, on the ride home, I informed Bishop of all the news that was shared. He did not recall the letter he wrote but was surprised that the refusal of burial by the local pastor was the needle in this haystack.

We were about seven minutes from the residence when he looked over at me and said, "John, did you know that Donna Brazile said this about the Church, 'It's not anti-Catholic to question, nor is it anti-Catholic to be honest about the previous shortcomings of the church, because that is the only way we can ensure its strength and dignity moving forward. It is, however, very Catholic to forgive each other and to never stop loving each other.' She is right, John, we have made mistakes, but if we cannot forgive and shower love on the other, we are not faithful followers of Jesus."

Bishop always surprised me with his memory. He could quote past and present persons just like that. I, on the other hand, would have to spend hours searching for the right quote to fit what I was writing or speaking about. In this case, I told the Boss that I had not heard or read Donna's statement but saw the truth in it.

Recently, I have questioned why he is always sharing with me things and views that are "above my pay grade"? They should be for men in his position. Even this week, he had me, as he always does, go over all the materials the Bishops' Conference had sent him. However, what was different was that he asked me to comment on each area as if I was the one who had to respond or vote on it. In the past, I have highlighted sections or made a note on the margin about a particular paragraph or the way it was worded. He did not want that this time, he wanted me to look at it with a bishop's eye. This was all so new to me and, I dare say, very strange.

That night at dinner, Bishop was suggesting that he begin a two-year series of parish visitation. He would like to spend a complete day in each parish. It would give him an opportunity of going over the sacramental and financial books of each parish. Plus, he would be able to meet the staff that works in our parishes. Bishop also wanted to be the celebrant of the morning or evening Liturgy so he could witness how many parishioners came out for it. I told him that I thought it was an ambitious project and not positive it could be done in two years. So many unplanned things or events happen that alter the schedule as it is now that we cannot always rearrange them. Adding full day visits would just compound the problem. The Boss said he would think about it, but that I should start working on a visitation schedule for him to approve. I knew the clergy in the diocese would not see this in the same light that Bishop did. Most would think he was spying on them or trying to find a reason to move them somewhere else.

We both commented, as we were eating our peach cobbler, with vanilla ice cream on top, how our two Order of the Cross members were getting along. Sister Agnes Gregory has added excitement and laughter. You often can hear from the kitchen or their living quarters the loud outburst of laughter by the two of them. Plus, she has really cut down the load of work for Sister Anesia. Let me tell you when Mary Jacoby is here you know it for sure. The laughter is louder, the talk more animated and the breaks seem a little longer. Knowing that they enjoy each other, being here, Bishop said made him feel secure that Mother Veronica, OC, would supply the house with sisters for years to come.

Bishop then told me: "John, always be aware of your staff and their needs. Know who takes care of you and where you work. From the janitor to your secretary know them well. If you want to know what is going on in your own building, they are the ones who will tell you." I wondered if he was considering replacing me with a new priest secretary and master of ceremonies. Possibly, he was thinking of naming me a pastor, and that is why all these personal talks about how I should interact and run a place. As always, I thanked the Boss for his advice, wondering why?

The next few days at the office I worked on the visitation list until I finally had all 205 parishes covered. Considering all the events already on his schedule I just did not see much wiggle room if something major occurred and demanded his time and presence.

I gave the plan to Rose, and she told me she would print out a copy and give it to Bishop for his approval or rejection.

Soon we will start the visitation to all our secondary schools for the Mass with the faculty and students. Actually, it will begin the day after Bishop returns from the Conference of Bishops. I had done as the Boss asked and written my own response to every paper that was to be discussed and how I would have voted and why. Bishop did ask me down to his room two nights ago. When I arrived, he had all my written responses before him. Bishop proceeded to tell me why my *no* vote should be a *yes* in five of the nine papers for the fall meeting. He asked me to stop thinking about what was best for this diocese, but rather for the Church in the USA. The living and working situations in the Mid-West, the deep South or the North West of the country demanded a more open approach. Each bishop has to be conscious of not only what is best for those he serves; but will the Church in the United States grow as a result of these policies or be forced to stay the same.

Bishop Harrington then handed me a piece of paper which he had Rose type and print out for me and was a quote by the late Pope Francis. It read,

"Despite the slowness, the infidelity, the errors and sins it committed and might still commit against its members, the Church, trust me, as no other meaning and goal but to live and witness Jesus."

Bishop just continued chatting making sure I understood that it was a Bishop's solemn obligation to be bearers of God's Word. Yes, at times to correct and admonish, but mostly to encourage those they were charged to look after with the desire to be like Christ in all things. To strive to live at peace with one another. To show love and compassion, not only to those they knew or who agreed with them but more so, to those who disagreed with them or showed hostility toward them. There was no place for petty grievances, grudges, or retaliation in the life of a bishop. Lead by example, as Pope Francis did, and now Pope James has been doing. They do not just write or speak about these things, they are living them out every day showing the Church and its leaders that it is possible. Most of today's bishops are not used to these expectations.

Bishop Harrington went on that being named a pastor, or a bishop is not to be seen as a promotion, honor, or recognition, but rather as a call to humility, service, compassion, and understanding. At that, I cut him off and asked him outright if he was planning on replacing me and making me a pastor? He looked at me and quickly informed me that he had no intention of replacing me, nor making me a pastor at this time. There would be a day when it would be right to appoint me pastor of one of our 205 parishes, but it was not today. The Boss went onto to say to me that he felt it was important for him to share with me what he has learned over the years. For six years now, we have worked beside one another, and he realized there was much he should be sharing with me. Plus, Bishop did not know how long before the cancer made it impossible for him to do his job.

Just then Fred pulled the car into the residence driveway and was getting out to open the door for Bishop. I told him, as we were starting to exit that I appreciated his honesty with me. We left it at that, and both went into the house and our respective rooms.

On Sunday evening Bishop took American Airlines to Philadelphia and then the transport service provided by the Marriott to check into his room and be ready for the start of the conference on Monday morning.

Bishop had studied and gone over again Sunday evening all the comments I had written and the reasons I gave for them. As he reread them for the last time, he found himself smiling with pride. He noted how I had picked up some of his expressions, ways of stating things and made them my own. The arguments were strong and theologically sound. The kind of argument a bishop should be capable of making. Bishop Harrington decided to use some of my arguments at the roundtable sessions they would have over these next days.

During the week, many of the bishops came up to him and told him they would be attending the concert, Liturgy, and dinner. He thanked them all and asked that they still return their invitation cards so the jubilee committee would have an accurate count. Only one of the cardinals had a conflict in schedule and would not be able to attend this time around. That still left four of them coming for our celebrations. Bishop was able to share with them that those involved had all been identified, but one was still elusive as to where he lived. Bishop was just happy that at this meeting they did not need all the security that had been present at their last national meeting. Things were getting back to normal again.

Upon his return, he told me that the meeting was a good one and that he had used some of my arguments at the roundtable sessions. Bishop

Harrington asked me to read the final documents coming out of the meeting. In particular, the bishops issued a revised medical ethics document. It now included a section on gene editing. Recently, in Oregon researchers had used CRISPR to actually change a gene in an embryo of a child that otherwise would have led to heart damage. The bishops have taken the position, at this time, that research should be monitored and restricted. It should not be used to alter secondary characteristics of the human person. Just because a family wants a blue-eyed, blond boy, the human embryo cannot be modified for such reasons. It should be restricted to disease prevention.

Bishop also said he had private meetings with both Cardinal Wolfgang and Cardinal McCormick. Bishop Harrington did not say what they were about and I knew better not to ask. Private means private!

The Papal Nuncio had responded that he would be able to make all three events and had been assured by Ricardo Cardinal Navarro, Papal Secretary of State that he planned on being present. This time it would be the Nuncio that would inform the state department when Cardinal Navarro's plane would be arriving and when he would be returning to Rome. The Nuncio also had a few questions that he wanted Bishop Harrington to respond to within the week. The Holy Father, Pope James, had requested the information through the Office of the Nuncio. That was all Bishop told me about the content of the Nuncio's letter to him.

I relayed the information to Detective Teeling about both the Nuncio and Secretary of State were coming again and staying with us. He told me that he would inform the Chief of Police and the house would be guarded again during their stay. Teeling asked me if we were going to be busing the bishops to the seminary again and I assured him that was the plan. The Police Department would provide the escort from the airport to the seminary. Plus, they would have escorts when they attended the different events. The Chief of Police felt the plan that had been worked out with the Federal Agencies involved for the last time, was a good one, and they all would be following it for this one. I asked Jimmy Teeling if they were any closer to knowing where Howard Thornton was yet? Unfortunately, they had not been able to find him.

However, one of the department foot patrol officers thought he saw someone that looked like the picture that had been distributed to all officers within the department. The man had been going into a pharmacy. By the time the young officer had called it in, and backup arrived this person had left and gone down to take the subway someplace. Maybe it was our missing Thornton person, perhaps it wasn't. If it was, it meant that he was here and that posed a grave risk for all the hierarchy attending our Jubilee celebrations. They had already notified the FBI and state department both of which were sending extra personnel to assist their department. I thanked him again for everything and said I would pass onto Bishop the latest news.

Bishop was in his office, so I went down, checked with Rose if he had anyone inside with him and she told me not right now. I proceeded to knock, and when I heard him tell me to enter, I went in and told him what Detective Teeling had shared with me. He thanked me for the update but reiterated his fear that innocent people might be hurt or killed if this person or the three of them tried something during one of the events. I reminded the Boss that both Sarah and James LaCross were being closely monitored so if they were to be involved we would have a warning of their movement. I knew the police would never let them get close to one of the events. What I had not considered is that either one of them or both would be used to distract law enforcement from the movement of Howard Thornton. Bishop still looked concerned, maybe even worried.

While I was in his office, I told Bishop this evening I would be going over to spend time with my three nephews. Kathy had called last night and suggested that I come over for dinner and spend some time with them. Bishop agreed and told me that I should work into my schedule time for them on a regular basis. Even if that meant not being here at the chancery as much, it seemed to Bishop during this time after their dad's death, my presence in their life would be much more meaningful. I thanked him for his sensitivity and assured him that I would take the extra time.

At dinner, the boys told me what they were up to at school, but the excitement was gone from their voices. I think the reality that their dad would never be home again, going to school events, sports practices, or just playing with them finally hit home. After dinner, we went outside and played ball in the yard for awhile. Then we took a break and just sat around the picnic table. I asked how they and their mom were making out. They told me that they could hear Mommy crying some nights and that made them very sad. Plus, Mommy was great, but she wasn't Daddy. She tried to do stuff with them that he did, but it just was not the same. I asked what kind of things? Guy stuff they told me. Like playing baseball, or cooking on the barbeque grill or fishing. Foolishly I said, I thought Mommy just the other night had cooked hamburgers and hot dogs on the grill for you. They looked at me and stated that she tried, but it was not like the way. Daddy did it.

He always made a production of his cooking on the grill. He would have them come over, tell him, by putting their hand over or touching the meat, when it was time to flip the burgers. Plus, he knew exactly the way they liked their hot dogs. Mommy tried, but she just didn't get it right. I asked the three of them if they would teach me how to do it. Their eyes got big and in unison shouted that they would. Then they wanted to know when? I told them that Bishop Harrington said I could spend more time with them and before I knew it they were hugging and squeezing me with all their might. Then I realized how much they were hurting not having my brother with them. And so, for the next six weeks, I did as promised. I spent a couple of days a week with them.

I was there when they came home from school, helped with homework, played ball, learned how to cook the way each boy liked, and helped put them to bed at night. Kathy and I in the process grew even closer. She appreciated every minute I spent with them. For one, it gave her time to do other things that needed to be done. She could leave the house knowing I was there, go to the beauty parlor, go shopping, or just visit with one of her girlfriends and get away for a couple of hours for time for herself. I was happy to be able to fill in and be there for her and the boys. As the weeks passed, both Kathy and I noticed how the boys were changing. They seemed more alive, happier again. They understood that I would not always be able to spend this much time with them, but they still liked the fact that I was with them now. I felt good and knew that my younger brother was looking favorably upon my effort.

One of the things the boys taught me was how to fish. Vic used to take them to one of the state parks, which had a slow river flowing through it, and each year, it was stocked with trout. I learned you could buy bait at this one store that sold fishing supplies and live bait. They showed me how to properly attach the bait, but also how to use different flys. Then we would stand along the edge and cast our lines in the hope of nailing that one big trout. In all honesty, we did not catch much. Only on one of those trips did we actually catch enough trout that Kathy was able to cook it for us that evening. It was not my favorite thing to do with them, but I learned as we stood along the river bank, the talk flowed more smoothly, they shared feelings more freely, and that was worth every minute I spent fishing.

I am proud of my nephews and the fine young men they are becoming. Kathy and Vic did an excellent job of imparting values, a sense of decency and respect in each of them. Plus, I learned while with them, the volunteer things each of them was doing. I had no idea that they were so involved giving back and being sensitive to those who did not have all that they did. My nephews were living the Gospel message, and I thanked God, my sister-in-law and brother for that.

Bishop and I were on the road revisiting the high schools. No applause when he entered his year, you could tell we were back to normal and the way things used to be. As usual, Bishop stayed for lunch with the faculty after each of the masses.

Two days a week, Fred drove Bishop Harrington to a different parish, and he would spend the day with them. In the evening, after they had dinner together, Bishop would share what he observed, possibly make some suggestions, but generally, let the pastors and their associates know that he found they were doing an excellent job. I did not go with him since my services really were not needed. When he celebrated Mass, he did not use his crozier or miter, and the local priests assisted during the Liturgy. On these days that he was not coming home for dinner, I would go to see and be with my nephews. On many of those evenings, my mom or Kathy's mom and dad would also be there. Kathy would always tell them when I would be present. It gave us grownups a chance to get caught up with one another.

This past week, Bishop, our superintendent of Catholic Schools, and the principal broke ground for what will be called Holy Angels Elementary School. The building that had the explosion and fire was torn down and now was the time to rebuild. We wanted to bring the students back to their own school. After the explosion and fire, our teachers who survived, as well as the students, were split up among our schools in the inner city. The additional students brought each building to its capacity. Classes were crowded, and parents complained. It will take just over a year to complete the new facility. Much of it is modular classrooms that are going to be assembled here on site. The Building and Sites department of the diocese found this would be the fastest and most economical way for the diocese to go. Our former teachers from here, as well as the principal, all had input into what the new classrooms and facilities will be like. They were excited to be asked to be part of the process. The school office has promised that they will all return to the new building, including those who were injured if they so desire. The new facility will be large enough to hold about one hundred more students than we could previously. This will help the principal expand our pre-K program. The modules come fully equipped, and there is a sprinkler system built-in so that need has also been addressed. Bishop has insisted that a memorial plaque is placed here, so we never forget the lives that were lost. The teachers suggested that it be in a memorial garden in the center courtyard of the new complex. That idea was accepted. With today's ceremony and the breaking of ground, the crews can come in and build the foundation on which the modular units will sit. The new building is also energy efficient and has its own solar panels on the roof, which will be capable of providing for all the electrical needs of the school.

It was just two weeks now before the celebrations for our 150th anniversary as a diocese were to take place. Once again the same catering company was hired to prepare the dinner. The joint choirs have been preparing for the jubilee concert. The Vicar-General had the Hilton secure for the Cardinals that would be able to attend. At our place, Sister Agnes Gregory, OC, had the rooms prepared for both the Papal nuncio and secretary of state. Everything was moving so smoothly it made me worry.

In the final week, all the law enforcement agencies that were working to protect the bishops had once again gone over every inch of the cathedral as well as the hall where the dinner was to be held. The staff of the catering company had all been vetted, and the owners were instructed that no change in personnel was now allowed. This time even the combined chorus was videotaped at their last practice, so clear images were captured of each member. The wine that would be consecrated during the

Mass was checked that no bottle had been tampered with and the wine box sealed and taped until the day of the Mass. As far as the agents and police assigned to protect during these days were concerned all they could do was now done. Everyone entering the cathedral would have to pass through metal detectors that had been brought in for that purpose.

The day before the concert is when most of the Bishops were arriving, as well as the Cardinals. The Nuncio and Secretary of State for the Vatican were scheduled to arrive in time for lunch on Friday. I knew that Bishop Harrington was going over to the seminary on Thursday night to greet all the bishops and make sure their accommodations were okay. That was another thing I would not be attending with him. It was just for the bishops.

Everything from this point on has happened so fast it is hard to recall all the details or even sequence of events. As Bishop was getting ready to go to the seminary, he came down to my room and asked me to join him. Naturally, I politely refused and reminded him that the only individuals who would be here were his fellow bishops. He just waved his hand and said that was not true. The rector of the seminary and some of the faculty would be present, so he wanted me to meet the bishops. I told him that the only reason the rector and some faculty were going to be present was that they were hosting all of them. The Boss just looked at me and said, "Get ready, John, we leave in twenty-five minutes and I don't want to be late." And with that, he turned and walked down the hall to his room. Totally puzzled by this change in plans, I put my best clerical suit on and was indeed ready when Fred pulled the car upfront. We stayed at the seminary, having cocktails, hors d'oeuvres with the assembled bishops for about two and a half hours. Bishop Harrington seemed to go out of his way to introduce me to each and every one of them. On the way back to the house, he informed me that tomorrow morning we would be going over to the Hilton to meet the five cardinals that had gathered.

I did not sleep well that night. Something just was not right. Six years I have been with this man, and the last couple of months, days I wondered who I was working for? Bishop Harrington was doing and sharing things with me like never before. I found it most unsettling, to say the least.

The next day, off we went to the hotel and met with the Cardinals. Everyone was on a first name basis but me. I called each one your Eminence or Cardinal when being introduced or greeting one of them. It was really only Cardinal McCormick our Metropolitan who I knew. They all told me to call them by their first name. Now that is strange. Priests do not call one of the members of the College of Cardinals by their first name. I don't even call Bishop Harrington by his first name after six years living and working with him. I felt totally out of place in this situation. Bishop Harrington, or Wally, as everyone in the room, was calling him just had this little smile on his face at my obvious discomfort. I was just happy when Wally said to the group he had to get back to the residence to be there when Archbishop Riossi the Papal Nuncio and Cardinal Navarro our Papal Secretary of State arrived at the house. Bishop did not want to put any pressure on the Sisters by not being there to greet our guests.

We were back in the house for all of maybe twelve minutes when I heard the police sirens coming down the street. The patrol cars brought the Nuncio's limo right up to the entrance of the house. Agents from the State Department charged with the Secretary's safety were out of their cars and in position when the limo came to a halt. Bishop and I were already coming down the front steps when the door was opened, and I got my first look at the feet of the secretary of state. He had, what had to be handmade, leather shoes on that were just magnificent. I then saw his red cassock appear as he lifted himself out of the car. Both men were in their respective cassocks. The Papal Secretary of State had rich black hair. It was said to be an influence of the ancient Aztec people of which his grandfather was descendent. He stood about five-foot-ten and had the warmest of smiles. One would say he had a kindly face. He put his hand out to greet Bishop Harrington and then me. Bishop shook hands with him, and I kissed his ring. At the moment, it just seemed to be the thing to do.

Then the Nuncio came around from the other side of the car and greeted Wally with an embrace as if they were old friends. The nuncio still has a solid Italian accent when he speaks. I was then introduced to him, and as I went to kiss his ring, he turned his hand, so we were forced to shake hands. He said to me as we were shaking hands, "It is indeed nice meeting you, I have heard a great deal about you." My legs began to shake. How the blazes had he, in Washington, DC, representing the Holy See to this country of ours, know anything about me. All I could manage to get out of my dry mouth was a thank you. At that, we all went inside the residence. I did note that for two men they seemed to have an abundance of luggage. I wondered if they were off to someplace else after being with us for two nights.

Sister Agnes Gregory showed them to their respective rooms. After about ten minutes, they were both downstairs and joined us in the sitting room. Bishop asked if they cared for anything but said no, they would wait for lunch.

After we had a light lunch, they asked Bishop
Harrington if they could meet with him. He took
them up in his study. I went to my room and fell
in my chair. The three of them had been together
about an hour now when my buzzer went off on
the phone. I picked it up, and Bishop asked if I
would come down to his study. I walked down
and entered. Bishop Harrington asked that I take a
seat. Once I was in the chair, he said that Cardinal
Navarro had something to say to me. I looked at
him and blurted out "to me?" The three prelates
just laughed. Cardinal Navarro said, "John, our
Holy Father, Pope James, has named you bishop
of the Ecclesiastical Province of Fermo outside of
Rome, and an appointment to the Congregation of
Faith." I believe, at that exact moment, my breathing
stopped. I just sat there staring at them, looking one
to the other, for some sign that this was a joke they
were playing on me. No one was showing any indi-
cation that this was a joke. Finally, I asked, "What
does this mean?" It was now Bishop Harrington
who filled me in. He said that Our Holy Father
wanted me in Rome immediately. There would be
no time for the usual public announcement that I
was bishop-designate and a scheduled ordination to
the Office of Bishop. It would happen tomorrow
morning, here in our chapel. By law, there have to
be three ordaining bishops, and I was told that the
Nuncio, the Secretary of State and himself would
be the three that I needed for a valid Ordination.

I just sat there, trying to absorb what he was saying but could not. Finally, it was Cardinal Navarro who spoke again and said that Pope James had been interested in me for some time.

It seems that Bishop Harrington had suggested my name for the office two years ago. It was not until this past year that the pope wanted to know about my work, my spiritual life, my commitment to ministry, but most importantly, my compassion for the poor, my ability to reach out to the marginalized, my ability to deal with other priests and religious. Bishop Harrington had been providing information to the Nuncio for months.

Bishop Harrington understood this was all coming as a shock to me. Matter of fact, he was shocked to learn that I would have to fly out to Rome on Monday. There would be no time for celebrations, those would have to come later when I returned home for a visit. Bishop told me he wanted me to call my mom and invite her to the ordination of her son as Bishop tomorrow morning at nine thirty. I was also to call Kathy and have her bring the boys. Bishop also wanted Valliere, her husband and girls to be present as well. I said that I did not know what to say. It was the Nuncio who suggested that I tell our Holy Father's representative Ricardo Cardinal Navarro that I accept. I looked at the Cardinal and told him to tell Pope James that I accepted but was not at all worthy or prepared for this office. Cardinal Navarro said that he would be making the call directly and inform the Pope of my decision and that I would be meeting with him on Tuesday in his office in the Vatican. I then said like a silly little kid, but I don't have anything to wear. I only own my black cassock and black clerical suit. Bishop Harrington told me that he had gone into my room while I was with my nephews and took all my sizes down. He then went into his bedroom and came out with a large box and handed it to me. Bishop said that it was okay for me to open it right now.

Inside I found a complete set of clothing, both formal and informal, that a bishop wears. Tears just started pouring down my face. This was all too much for me. Not only the news that I was now bishop-designate, and tomorrow noon would be an actual Bishop, but that Bishop Harrington had done all this without me knowing it. What I held in my hands would have cost him a small fortune, and he was handing it as his ordination gift to me. I put the box down, and with tears still running down my face, held this man in my arms and thanked him over and over again. When we broke apart, he told me to take the box, go make the phone calls, and then come downstairs and join your colleagues for celebratory drinks before dinner and tonight's concert.

I made the calls to my family members. My mom screamed, my sister Vallierie, and sister-in-law Kathy were just stunned and said nothing before screaming into the phone. All agreed that tomorrow morning they would be here to witness my Ordination as Bishop.

While we were having dinner, Bishop said that tonight I would still wear my black cassock to the concert, but at tomorrow's Mass and dinner, I would wear my Bishop's cassock. He would, with the permission of the Nuncio and Cardinal after introducing them at the start of the Mass, make the official announcement that I had been ordained bishop and would be leaving for Rome on Monday morning.

The Secretary of State had brought along with him all the necessary documents that I would have to sign as well as the official document naming me bishop with the signature of Pope James and his seal attached. The Nuncio and Bishop Harrington would witness my Profession of Faith.

I know I went to the jubilee concert and believe it was a success. I just have no recollection of that evening. My mom who had purchased a ticket to the concert was all over me after it. We hugged, we cried, especially when I told her I had to leave for Rome on Monday. I told her what Bishop Harrington had given me as a gift for my ordination and she cried again. Where do all these tears come from? The two of us spent more time crying and holding each other than talking. Finally, Mom went home to try and sleep, I knew there would be very little for me.

The next morning, I was out of bed and showered by 6:30 AM. I have dressed in a white collarless shirt with french cuffs and plain gold cufflinks. Black trousers, black socks, and shoes when I went down for breakfast. The other three clerics were already up and dressed in their respective cassocks. The three of them went over the ordination rite with me. Bishop had called Father Peter last evening and told him to be here this morning and be our master of ceremonies. He also instructed Peter to go over the Rite of Ordination of a Bishop and make sure he knew the order backward and forward. That meant Father Peter probably had little or no sleep last evening.

Peter arrived at the residence at 8:00 AM. Bishop had Sister Agnes take him right up to the chapel and set everything out. Sister Anesia supplied the apron Bishop Harrington would wear when anointing me. Lemons were cut for the washing of our hands after the Sacred Chrism had been used. My family arrived in two cars at nine o'clock. I came down stairs in my bishop's cassock to greet them and immediately they crying started. My oldest nephew Baron brought everyone back to reality when he said, "Now don't you just look pretty in that new dress, like the color on you Uncle Jack, or do I have to call you Uncle Bishop Jack now?" Everyone laughed, and I told him Uncle Jack was still okay with me and always would be.

At nine thirty, the mass of Ordination of a Bishop began. We did not finish until 11:00 AM. Cardinal Navarro had brought from Rome, as a gift from the Pope, my Bishop's ring. The Nuncio, not wanting to be left out, had purchased a wooden crozier made of cherry wood and crafted by the Trappist monks for me. The Secretary of State announced that he would be installing me as bishop of the Ecclesiastical Province of Fermo the Sunday after my arrival. He also presented me with my appointment to the Congregation of Faith, signed by Pope James. At the conclusion of the Liturgy, I gave my blessing to each member of my family. Pictures were taken, documents signed, when Bishop announced that we had about twenty minutes before we would have to leave and go to the cathedral to celebrate the jubilee mass.

It was decided that the Papal Secretary of State and Nuncio would ride in the car provided by the State Department. Bishop and I would be taken over by Fred. When I walked out the front door, and Fred saw me dressed in my choir cassock with pectoral cross hanging from my neck and a gold ring on my finger his mouth just dropped open. Bishop Harrington broke the silence and introduced Bishop John Writerson to Fred. Fred, to my utter embarrassment, genuflected, and kissed my ring, got up, and gave me the tightest bear hug of my life. Bishop Harrington burst out laughing and told Fred that he would personally tell him all about it next week, but now we had to get to the church on time. Fred started to go over to open Bishop's door as he has for six years when he stopped, opened mine, and then took Bishop Harrington around the other side and let him into his usual place in the backseat of the car. Bishop Harrington just looked at me and said, "Get used to it, John, in Rome with your working for the Congregation of Faith, the attention is only going to get worse." I knew he was right, but for now, it all seemed like a dream to me.

The Nuncio and Secretary of State arrived before us and were already dressed for Mass in the hall off the sacristy. The Nuncio had already announced to all the 150 or so bishops from around the country that I had been ordained a Bishop that morning by himself, the Papal Secretary of State and Bishop Harrington at the direct order of the Pope James who was calling me to work in the Congregation of Faith. He also announced that I would be leaving on Monday for my new positions. As a result, when Bishop Harrington and I arrived everyone knew. As soon as I walked into the room, they burst into applause. Everyone seemingly coming at me in mass to congratulate me, welcome me into membership of the National Conference of Bishops and wish me well in Rome. It was a very heady experience for a man, who just twenty-four hours before was a mere priest secretary and MC to the Ordinary of Wallington. Now I was one of them, a member of the hierarchy of the Roman Catholic Church in the United States. Just as my head stopped spinning you could hear the sound of the organ, the choir starting to sing the entrance song, and before I knew it, the procession was moving forward and into the Cathedral. Behind the Cross and two candle bearers came the priests of the diocese, followed by the Bishops of this country. Bishop Harrington had me last in the line of Bishops and just before the Cardinals. They were followed by the Papal secretary of state and lastly Bishop Harrington. He processed down the aisle with his head held high, crozier in hand knowing this was his cathedral, his flock and proud as a peacock about my elevation to the Episcopacy. Everyone reverenced the altar, and Bishop Harrington went over to his chair under his coat of arms.

When the singing stopped, he began the Eucharistic celebration with the sign of the Cross. He then welcomed all who had gathered for this special occasion of our diocese. He acknowledged our local civic leaders the mayor and governor, the religious leaders of other churches especially Most Reverend Henry Wallis of the Episcopal diocese who was using this church till their repairs were complete, the cardinals he introduced individually and thanked them, as well as all the bishops who had come here today. Then he said he wished to present to the people of the Diocese of Wallington, his former master of ceremonies and priest-secretary the newly ordained bishop and latest member of the Congregation of Faith, their very own bishop, the Most Rev. John Writerson, DD. After a moment of stunned silence, the Cathedral broke into spontaneous applause. I even saw Detective Jimmy Teeling clapping for all he was worth. Bishop motioned for me to come to the microphone. I went over, first to embrace him and then to say a few words in thanks. As I reached my mentor and friend, he put his hands out to greet me, and I put mine out to embrace him.

At that moment as people were clapping and staring at us, Howard R. Thornton stepped out of the confessional on the left side of the cathedral. Semi-automatic rifle in hand, he raised it. As he did, a parishioner at the end of the aisle saw the movement and without thinking, jumped out and lunged himself at the man. He caught Thornton's right leg and started to pull him down just as he fired the first shot. The bullet hit me squarely in the chest, and I fell back instantly.

Epilogue

My name is William Harrington. I am the Ordinary of the Diocese of Wallington. Last week, the late Bishop John Writerson's mom handed me a journal. It contained what you have been reading. After John's death and funeral, his things at the residence were packed up and given to his family. It took a period of time before his mother could even go through them. In the process, she discovered this journal and felt it did not belong to the family, but it belonged to the diocese or me. I have spent the last week reading through it and felt that the story it told should be published.

I called a dear friend of mine who is a publisher and asked him to read through it. If he agreed that it was of value for people to read, would his company publish it as a lasting tribute to one of the best priest friends a bishop could ever have?

My former priest secretary and master of ceremonies died in my and his mother's arms. We held him there in the sanctuary as he took his last breath. Gert's oldest and only son left was now dead. No mother should ever have to endure such pain as losing two sons in less than a year.

The newspaper ran a large print headline the next morning. It read, "Bishop Murdered." John's body was brought back to the Cathedral for his Wake. Attired in this Episcopal cassock and mass vestments, with his white Miter on his head, pectoral cross lying on his chest, and Bishop's ring on his finger, thousands passed by his body to pay their final respects. Pope James sent a handwritten letter to Mrs. Writerson thanking her for the gift of her son to the church and telling her why he wanted him in Rome. It was a moving and consoling letter that she cherishes.

Once a month, I have his Mom Gert over for dinner with me. She needed someone to vent with, and I needed her. In her I see John, and together we talk, mourn, share stories about him, and some nights even find ourselves laughing again. His death bonds us to one another. Let me also share with you, as I did with his mom, that my cancer is in remission.

I can tell you that Howard Thornton was convicted of first-degree murder. Sarah Mitchell is Howard Thornton's sister, and the two of them have hated me ever since I denied their father's burial and refused to see them for more than the customary fifteen minutes. James LaCross met Thornton in prison, and they became best friends. Sarah and James were found guilty of conspiracy to commit murder. In a separate trial, Sarah Mitchell was convicted of attempted murder. I testified at their trials and am satisfied with the decision of the jury. John Writerson was the greatest priest secretary and master of ceremonies I ever had. He was only a bishop for a couple of hours before taking a bullet meant for me.

After Bishop Writerson's body had been removed from the Cathedral, the jubilee mass did go on. The Papal Secretary of State delivered a short version of his message from Pope James. At the time for the homily, I only told the people I would break down if I tried to preach and hoped they understood. Our 150th jubilee became a somber affair. The dinner did go on that evening. The Nuncio thanked the people for giving the Universal Church one of its sons in Bishop Writerson and that his death was a great tragedy, not only for us but for the whole Church.

Many of the Bishops came back a week later for John's funeral mass. I was the Principal Celebrant of the Eucharistic Liturgy and now ask you to join with me in prayer for a man who loved the Priesthood of Jesus.

Lord, give your mercy and love to John, your servant and bishop. He hoped in Christ and preached Christ. May he share with Christ the joy of eternal life. We ask this through Christ, our Lord. Amen.

I also wrote the last page of John's journal dialogue, in his style, so you knew what happed that fateful day.

Acknowledgments

Quotations attributed to individual writers were obtained from Brainyquotes.Com.

Front cover picture from Pexels.com.

The author is indebted to my longtime friend, Christopher Poh, for his invaluable insights, critique, and suggestions for improvements. A gifted writer and gentle soul in his own right that you could ever meet.

Any errors in content or format are mine alone.

Finally, I would like to thank the editorial staff from Covenant Books for their expertise and assistance in preparing this work for publication.

About the Author

Rev. Dr. John G. Pisarcik has given retreats, workshops, seminars both nationally and internationally.

Most of Father John's active ministry was in the field of education. He has taught at all levels from elementary to graduate schools. He served as Principal of both private and regional high schools, taught Moral Theology in a graduate school of theology. He also was Director of Ministry programs at the college level and a member of the summer faculty for doctoral candidates at university level. He holds a Bachelor's degree, two Master's degrees, and a Doctorate in Sacred Theology/Ministry.

Dr. Pisarcik was ordained in 1970. Today he has Multiple Sclerosis, which limits his movements, speech, and is retired.

Previously published books of his are the following:

Ramblings of an Old Man

Hard Choices for Christians: A Collection of Contemporary Essays

Naughty or Nice—Virtue or Vice: Which will it be?

His books may be obtained from the CreateSpace store.com., Amazon.com or Kindle.com.